STAINED GLASS

STAINED GLASS

TECHNIQUES & PROJECTS

Mary Shanahan

GUILD OF MASTER CRAFTSMAN PUBLICATIONS

First published 2001 by
Guild of Master Craftsman Publications Ltd
Castle Place, 166 High Street,
Lewes, East Sussex BN7 1XU

Text © Mary Shanahan 2001
© in the work GMC Publications 2001
Photographs by Chris Skarbon and Anthony Bailey, except on pp. 2-3
(Courtesy The Ancient Art & Architecture Collection Ltd).

The publishers wish to thank Opus Stained Glass of Poynings
in West Sussex for their help in demonstrating the techniques described
by the author, and Chris Skarbon for his photographic contribution
throughout the publishing process.
The author was especially grateful to Kevin Woodgate for his expertise in
preparing the original draft of this book.

ISBN 1 86108 196 0

A catalogue record for this book is available from the British Library.

Edited by David Arscott
Cover designed by Ian Hunt Design
Book designed by Lovelock & Co
Drawings by Penny Brown © GMC Publications

Set in Albertus and Meta

Colour origination by Viscan Graphics (Singapore)
Printed in Hong Kong by H & Y Printing Ltd

Contents

Section 2

PROJECTS

Section 3

ADVANCED PROJECTS

Section 4

HINTS, TIPS AND REFERENCE

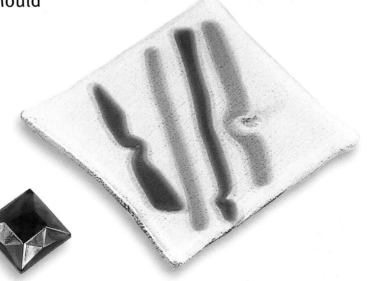

Introduction

THE HISTORY OF STAINED GLASS

Stained glass has been used to beautify our buildings for at least a thousand years, and for an artist who works in the medium it is almost impossible to imagine a world without it. Some of the oldest remaining pieces date back to the eleventh century and can be found in Augsburg, Bavaria. By the twelfth century stained glass was being used extensively in the decoration of Gothic cathedrals. Wells, Salisbury and Winchester in England, Chartres and Amiens in France – as well as Notre Dame in Paris – Cologne in Germany and Toledo in Spain are just a few of the many built about this time.

The use of large stained glass windows had two functions: first, to enhance the actual appearance of the place of worship by allowing the light flowing through the windows to create patterns of shimmering colours, thereby transforming the otherwise dull stone walls and aisles; secondly, as didactic tools: depicting passages of the Bible, they taught the worshippers in a visual way which would be easily remembered. Later in the twelfth century Cistercian abbeys were forced by a decree of their Order to have only clear glass in their windows. It is generally believed that this was because there was a need to make the abbeys less decorative, in order that there be less distraction from serious prayer and meditation. Following this decree, glass tinted to a lesser degree than previously, and also cheaper to produce, began to be used in other places of worship. This glass was widely used in grisaille windows, the beauty of which lay in their muted delicate colours.

The thirteenth century saw the introduction of medallion and rose windows, this latter a circular window characterized by abstract designs as well as figures. It was during this century, too, that the use of lead in the pictures became less extensive and clear glass began to be painted.

In the fourteenth century silver stain (silver oxide) was discovered and it was employed to tint glass from palest yellow to deepest orange. Also, at about this time, flashed glass began to be used: by putting one colour on another while the glass was still in a molten state, a second and third streak of colour was produced in the glass. Great painting experiments were also undertaken during the fourteenth century, and York Minster possesses some beautiful examples.

The fifteenth century witnessed the demise of lead as the sole outlining device for figures and designs in the windows. More often details were painted in, the lead's intervention in the desired pattern being completely ignored. Artists began to design stained glass. Soon the streaming light shining through traditional stained glass was lost as more and more glass was painted, blocking out the light.

Stained glass was no longer exclusively used in churches and cathedrals but also came to be employed in a domestic environment.

In the sixteenth century the Dutch produced many of the most notable works in stained glass. Bernard van Orley, who studied painting under Raphael, designed stained glass windows for a number of cathedrals in Holland and Belgium. The work of several of his pupils still exists in Brussels and Amsterdam.

In England, too, when the Renaissance took hold, stained glass came to be much in demand. However, the work was mainly undertaken by Dutch and Flemish painters who settled in England. One of the finest examples of their work can be seen in King's College Chapel, Cambridge. The painting on the glass is superb. Meanwhile in Spain stained glass windows continued to be created for cathedrals, notable examples being those in Seville and Toledo.

Sadly the sixteenth century dealt a death blow to stained glass and, indeed, to many other forms of art in places of worship. In England the Reformation brought about widespread destruction of stained glass in

Reims Cathedral, France: Great rose window/West front, 13th century

churches and cathedrals. In the Netherlands the Calvinists and in Germany Lutheranism had the same effect on ecclesiastical stained glass as the Protestants had in England.

After this devastation religious themes and characters were no longer used as subjects for stained glass; heraldry and non-biblical stories began to appear. The use of perspective was now more predominant and, at the same time, small stained glass panels were made to order for use in houses.

There was a great decline in stained glass during the seventeenth and eighteenth centuries. Coloured glass was scarce and expensive. Increasingly, plain glass windows were painted instead. The brothers William and Joshua Price were amongst the best-known and sought-after glass painters of the eighteenth century. They worked on many of the windows for the colleges of Oxford. Another glass painter of note during this period was William Peckitt, who painted windows for Oxford and Cambridge colleges, Exeter Cathedral and York Minster.

After its decline in the seventeenth and eighteenth centuries stained glass enjoyed an enormous revival during the nineteenth. Artists and craftsmen once again became interested in experimenting with textures and colours of glass. Charles Winston in England experimented extensively to produce glass as bright and clear in colour as medieval glass had been. It was he who produced what we know today as antique glass.

King Ine and Egbert windows, Wells Cathedral, England, 13th century

Thus, over the centuries, the technology of stained glass windows had turned full circle: in the nineteenth cenury, artists were once again using coloured glass to enrich their designs, rather than relying on the application of enamel. William Morris & Co. was the most respected stained glass firm in England during the latter part of the century.

At the same time researchers in the United States were seeking to improve the quality of glass colour. Their experiments, instead of achieving purer colour, discovered what we now know as opalescent glass. In that the streaks of opaque in the glass actually kept out the light, this actually countered the original aim of true stained glass. Louis Comfort Tiffany, who was involved in this research, used opalescent glass to produce ornate lampshades. Because of the many small curves in their design, metal channelling replaced traditional came as a border for the glass. Nowadays copper-foil is used.

Although, at the end of the nineteenth century, stained glass was much in demand, it suffered another decline in popularity at the beginning of the twentieth. Art Nouveau, with its pretty designs of fruit and flowers, had grown and virtually vanished within the space of two decades.

Some rather abstract stained glass was produced during the twentieth century, although its historical significance has yet to be determined. A modern building of steel and concrete lends itself to this type of stained glass, the materials and the decoration working sympathetically with one another. Dalle de verre – the method by which large pieces of slab glass are embedded in either concrete or epoxy resin – is also used a great deal in modern buildings. Buckfast Abbey in Devon, where three complete walls have been decorated in this way, stands as a magnificent example of the technique. The east wall depicts Christ with outstretched arms, a most impressive and colourful window, while one side wall has predominantly red and orange glass depicting day, and the other blue and green to signify night.

After a period in the twentieth century during which few studios used it in the execution of their stained glass commissions, painting on glass is now making a comeback, with a growing number of ready-mixed glass-painting pigments available. The use of another twentieth-century discovery, fused glass (in which coloured glass is fused on to another glass to form a design), is also becoming more extensive.

Controversy always accompanies any deviation from tradition when there are major commissions for stained glass windows. At the time of their consecration in 1962, for example, the new Coventry Cathedral windows were much criticized by traditionalists. With time, however, they and other modern stained glass windows have been accepted, not as a replacement for traditional stained glass, but as illustrations of an added dimension in the use of coloured glass.

TYPES OF GLASS

1 Antique glass is perhaps the glass most frequently used. It is also the most varied. Being handmade, it is characterized by streaks, ripples, bubbles and other irregularities which add to its beauty. The glass itself is not old, but it is termed 'antique' because it is the glass closest in type to that used centuries ago.

2 Flashed stained glass is a type of antique glass. It has a light-coloured base glass which is, as the name suggests, flashed with deeper colours. The resultant streaks of light and dark are most attractive.

3 Cathedral glass is much cheaper than antique glass and is therefore the type generally used by the hobbyist. Machine-rolled, it is sometimes textured on one side and smooth on the other. The textures include rippled and hammered. Seedy glass contains bubbles. Cathedral glass has a uniform thickness of about 3mm (⅛in) and is extremely easy to cut.

4 Opalescent glass is a mixture of colours swirled together and is machine-made. As the name implies, it is slightly opaque.

5 Fused glass is used less frequently because a kiln is required for this process.

6 Globs, **7 roundels**, **8 jewels** and **9 lenses** are used for decoration. Roundels are made by twirling molten glass blobs and then allowing them to flatten. Jewels are small molten pieces of glass used as decoration.

Dalle de verre (slab glass) refers to glass cut in thick slabs approximately 25mm (1in) thick, and usually the slabs are either 30 x 30cm (12 x 12in) or 30 x 20cm (12 x 8in). It is commonly used in modern buildings where pieces are embedded in concrete or epoxy resin.

Getting started

With modern materials and techniques it is quite possible for the layman to take up stained glass as a hobby, and it is with the beginner in mind that I have written this book. After you have mastered the techniques, and have come to know the feel and beauty of stained glass by undertaking some of the following projects, I hope you will consider taking up the art of stained glass at a more advanced level.

BASIC TOOLS AND EQUIPMENT

1 fume trap	*7* oil-filled cutter	*12* horse-shoe nails
2 cut-running pliers	*8* steel wheel cutter	*13* brush
3 grozing pliers	*9* tallow	*14* hammer
4 cutting square	*10* oyster knife	*15* electric soldering iron in stand
5 brush for flux	*11* Nova tool for opening and	*16* lead vice
6 lead knife	closing lead came	

You will need various tools and other items before you start, including a **board** on which to work. Chipboard is suitable. It must be at least 50mm (2in) larger than your work all round. When you are working with lead your board will also need to have a raised wooden border along the bottom and up the left-hand side.

Good ventilation is essential, and a **fume trap** for absorbing fumes and vapour created by solder and flux (1, facing page) is ideal if you can afford it. Here are some of the other tools you will find yourself using on a regular basis.

Cut-running pliers (2) used for breaking glass after it has been scored with your cutter.

Grozing pliers (3) a specialist tool for nipping off small jagged pieces of glass. Ordinary pliers do not grip the glass as well.

Cutting square (4) for scoring straight lines on the glass.

Small brush (5) for applying flux (child's watercolour brush will do).

Lead-cutting knife (6) specialist knives can be expensive, and I have found that a small, sharp knife such as a Stanley knife is adequate.

Glass cutter (7,8) single-wheel cutters are obtainable at most glass merchants. Start with a steel-wheel cutter, which is the cheapest option. Only when you have decided that you like working with glass is it worth buying a tungsten-wheel cutter. These wheels make glass cutting very easy. Also on the market are super cutters with inbuilt reservoirs for the wheel lubricating oil or white spirit.

SAFTY NOTES

ALWAYS wear protective eyewear when cutting glass (ordinary spectacles or weak coloured sunglasses are adequate), or when using liquid flux: if the flux has been too liberally applied the hot solder sometimes spits.

DO NOT leave pieces of glass overlapping the edge of your bench or worktable. ALWAYS clear away small pieces of glass systematically while you are working.

NEVER lean on a bench where glass has been cut unless it has been swept clean: most cuts are caused by people resting their hands on small slivers of glass.

Oyster knife (10) for pushing strips of lead came into position around glass.

Nova tool or **lathekin** (11) a wedge-shaped tool used for opening came.

Horseshoe nails (12) and **hammer** (14) for securing leadwork.

Scrubbing brush (13) for applying cement/putty.

Soldering iron (15) 75 watt or 100 watt. Ideally, if you can afford it, you should buy a 100 watt temperature-controlled soldering iron with stand.

Vice (16) to hold the end of the lead while you are stretching it straight. A special lead vice is not necessary: any vice will serve the purpose.

SPECIALIZED TOOLS AND EQUIPMENT

As you gain confidence and begin to attempt more complicated projects you will want to add to your tools:

Glass grinder (below) one of the most useful tools to acquire. While it is possible to snap off small jagged pieces of glass with grozing pliers, it is not easy to make the edges completely smooth. After you have cut off the bulk of the glass it is possible to follow very precise patterns and curves with a grinder. It also leaves the edges very smooth. As stained glass becomes increasingly popular so grinders are becoming more hobby oriented and a small grinder is not too expensive. A very worthwhile investment.

Stand or **Easel** a simple wooden construction which allows you to paint your glass with daylight shining directly through it, giving you an accurate feel for the finished project as you work. You can also attach pieces of glass to the base glass of the stand (using Plasticine or Blu-tack) if you want to check or make decisions about colour schemes for any of your projects. (On the opposite page I show you how to make your own.)

I also strongly recommend a **light box** – a box lit from within and 'lidded' with frosted glass (see page 12 for making your own). This helps you to assess your colours as you work.

Grinder, with glass laid against the grinding head

Make your own stand or easel for glass painting

A glass stand or easel is easy to make. This model is a very simple construction (see diagram) and when not in use can be folded flat so that it does not take up much space.

If you usually paint with your work in a horizontal position, it is advisable to practise painting glass in a vertical position on your stand, and to use a piece of waste glass rather than attempting a real project with no experience of your equipment.

METHOD

1 Take an old wooden picture frame, preferably about 61 x 91cm (24 x 36in), and fit a piece of plain glass into it at the back and secure it with small wooden strips. The glass should be 4mm minimum, with a plastic safety film beneath.

2 On the front, about 50mm [2in] up from the bottom, make a small shelf to support your work while you are painting: attach a piece of wood, with a raised batten nailed to the front of it, to the frame.

3 Attach two legs with hinges so that they can be folded in when the stand is not in use. Attach a crossbar between the legs in order to stabilize the stand.

4 Screw eyelets to both the legs and the front of the stand. Thread a string through these eyelets and tie it off – to hold the stand secure when it is in the open position.

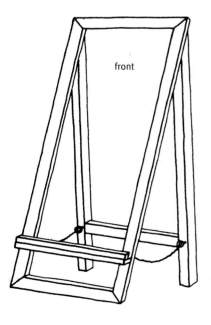

front

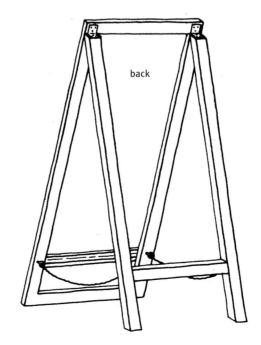

back

Make your own light box

MATERIALS

Wood for base 67 x 46cm (26½ x 18in)

2 pieces white plastic-covered board for short sides 42 x 75cm (16½ x 3in)

2 pieces white plastic-covered board for long sides 67 x 7.5cm (26½ x 3in)

Sandblasted or frosted glass for top (at least 6mm, an ideally with transparent plastic safety film dunderneath) 67 x 46cm (26½ x 18in)

4 rubber feet (not required if to be hung permanently on wall)

Metal corners to secure top to sides

A light box can be used for two purposes: to assess your colours while you are constructing a panel and as a permanent fixture behind a panel to illuminate it. This is extremely effective to lighten up a dark hall or a wall away from a window.

Fluorescent tubes need special control gear with a choke and starter switch. I have found that standard domestic daylight tubes can easily be adapted to suit the requirements of a light box.

METHOD

1 Make up the box leaving off top glass panel. Drill three ventilation holes 2cm (¾in) in diameter in each side.

2 Paint the inside base of the box white if dark wood has been used, using heat-resistant paint.

3 Secure three fluorescent tubes to base with spring clips. Attach the switch to the side of the box. Attach cable with a 13 amp plug. Remove the 13 amp fuse and replace it with 5 amp fuse.

4 Place the glass on top of the box and secure it with metal corners. Note: the glass has to be fairly opaque to diffuse the light of the fluorescent tubes.

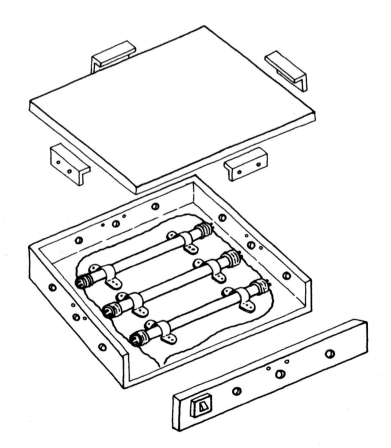

RAW MATERIALS

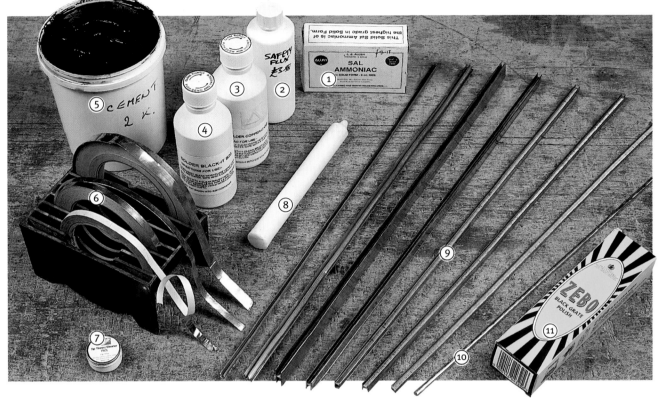

Use white spirit, fine-grade machine oil or a mixture of light oil and paraffin (two parts paraffin to one part any oil or white spirit) as a **lubricant** for your cutting wheel. Saturate a ball of cotton wool or foam, place it in a small screw-top jar, and then dip the cutter wheel into the mixture at regular intervals as you cut the glass.

Sal ammoniac (1) and (7) for cleaning and tinning your soldering iron.

Flux for soldering, either liquid (2) or paste. You can also use **tallow** (8) for lead work.

Patina (3, 4) obtainable from craft shops for colouring the solder.

Lead light cement (5) for cementing and weatherproofing leaded panels.

Copper foil (6) in widths from 4mm to 10mm.

Lead came (9, seven strips shown) obtainable from all stained-glass stockists and some glaziers, is generally sold in 2m (6½ft) lengths. Most of your work with traditional windows and panels will be with **H came** The most useful width to start with is 6mm (¼in): if you buy anything narrower your glass cutting must be very accurate. Wider came (10mm [⅜in]) is generally used for the outside borders of a window to provide added strength, though it is also possible to purchase steel-reinforced lead to strengthen any large works. H came can be round or flat: it is merely a case of choosing which type best suits a particular panel. The inside is usually referred to as the heart of the came. **C came** is used for edging panels. **Corner came** (usually called angled lantern lead in the trade) is a relatively modern type of came, giving a clean edge to the right-angled sides of large terrariums and boxes. It is more difficult to use: practise on waste glass first!

Solder (10) stick solder is easiest to handle. The cheapest is 40/60 (40 tin: 60 lead), known as plumber's solder and suitable for leadwork, while 50/50 can be used for all stained glass work, including lampshade-making.

Zebrite (11) to blacken leads.

HOW TO CUT GLASS

Before you embark on your first project you should practise just cutting glass. Always wear eye protection, even if it is just ordinary spectacles or 'light' sunglasses.

It is not possible to cut a shape 'out of' a piece of glass as you would from cloth: once you have started a cut, you have to continue it to the edge. The diagrams below show the cuts you would need to make in order to achieve the shapes at the centre of each piece of glass.

- Use a single-wheel cutter (see Basic Tools and Equipment, page 8) and clear, cheap horticultural glass.

- Spread several layers of newspaper on a steady table or bench.

- To begin with, lay a simple design comprising only straight lines under clear glass.

- Grasp the cutter between your index finger and middle finger (supported underneath by your thumb) and pull it along the glass with just enough pressure so that you can hear a scoring sound. If you find it difficult to hold the cutter between your index and middle finger, try holding the cutter as you would a pencil (see photograph). Do not press so hard that the glass flakes at the edges of the cut.

- Use a ruler backed with a piece of rubber (to stop it slipping) to guide your cutter along the glass.

HOW TO CUT GLASS — BASIC METHOD

Dotted lines show the cuts necessary to achieve the shapes chosen for the design

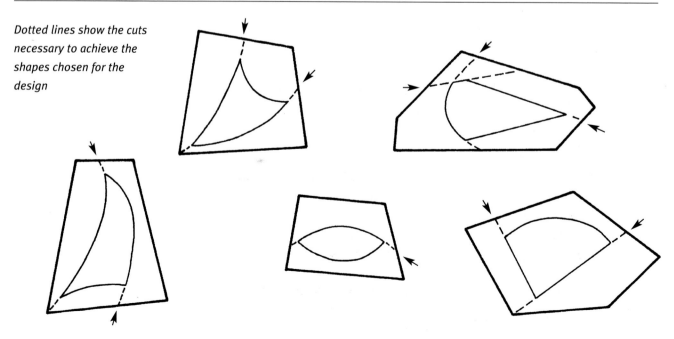

- Snap the glass apart along the scored line. Do not worry if you feel at first that you will not be able to manage this: if you lay the scored line over a pencil and push the cut piece of glass down firmly, it will snap. Alternatively, if you tap under the scored line with the ball end of your cutter, you will see the score 'run' and the glass break. This was the traditional way to cut curved lines. The modern equivalent is to use cut-running pliers (as used for tile cutting): having placed the jaws of the pliers over the score line, squeeze the handles together and the glass will break.

- Keep practising the cutting of straight lines and curves until you find it really easy.

- When you are cutting tight inner curves, you will have to score your waste glass (i.e. the glass you do not require) and gradually remove it with grozing pliers.

Professionals hold the cutter between the index and middle finger, but use a pencil grip (as here) if you find that more comfortable.

After scoring a straight line you can usually snap the glass with your fingers.

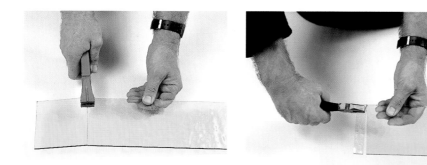

An alternative is to use cut-running pliers. Squeeze the end of the scored line and the glass will break cleanly along its length.

Grozing pliers are used a) for narrow ends of glass which would require considerable strength to snap by hand, and b) to break off glass bit by bit around tight curves.

COPPER-FOILING

Copper-foil self-adhesive tape is sold in many widths and can be purchased from craft shops. When you first start to use it, and especially when making terrariums, it is best to buy the 5mm ($^7/_{32}$in) width. This will allow for slight errors in your glass cutting.

Cut a corner out of the copper-foil packet and pull about 200mm (8in) of foil from the roll at a time. Remove the backing paper and wrap your glass in the foil so that the edges extend evenly each side of the glass. (See below.) Keep both glass and foil as clean as possible because the foil will not stick on dirty glass. To be sure, you can clean your glass with methylated spirits.

Press the foil over the edges of the glass with your fingers, and then rub a pen or pencil along the foil, pressing it down hard to make it adhere firmly to the glass. If the foil does not stick really well, do not continue with your work, because it will later fall apart.

Note Copper-foiling techniques are illustrated in the mirror-backed terrarium project on page 20.

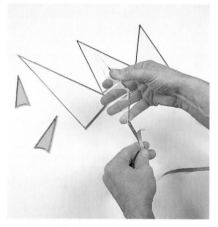

Wrapping copper-foil round the edges of the glass.

Rubbing a pen along the foil so that it adheres firmly to the glass.

TINNING

Apply flux to the copper foil with a small brush. Touch your solder with a hot soldering iron so that a blob of the solder falls onto the foil. Drop blobs of solder about 10cm (4in) apart along the foil. Run your hot soldering iron over the foil, from blob to blob, and the solder will flow over the flux and tin the foiled edges. (See page 22.)

SOLDERING

All soldering (other than spot soldering) must be done with the seam you are soldering in a horizontal position. Wipe your soldering iron frequently on a wet rag while you are working, in order to keep it clean. (See page 22.)

Many people find it easier, when working on three-dimensional objects, to solder the sides on top of the base – rather than outside it – because the spot soldering can be done from the outside. In appearance, however, the object looks slightly neater when the sides are attached to the outside. If you do decide to place the sides outside the base, note that soldering must begin from the inside. It is worth experimenting to see which you prefer.

SEAM SOLDERING
Flux adjoining pieces of foiled and tinned glass. Apply your solder as described for tinning, running it along between blobs. You now have a flat seam joining your pieces together.

BEAD SOLDERING
The seam solder leaves a flat join, whereas the bead join leaves a raised solder line. To bead solder, apply more flux and solder to your seamed join and then run the soldering iron along about 3mm (⅛in) above the solder until you have a slightly raised soldering line.

Projects

This section offers you the opportunity to create a variety of decorative and useful objects using a range of stained glass techniques – copper-foil, appliqué and traditional lead came. The projects vary in difficulty, but they are all suitable for the enthusiastic beginner.

Once you have produced some of these objects and feel confident using the techniques, you may like to try some of the more advanced pieces featured in the Advanced Section (see page 77).

COPPER-FOIL AND ART NOUVEAU

For many centuries stained glass was thought of mainly in relation to church and cathedral windows, and it was certainly in these settings that it was shown to best advantage. Gradually, however, it moved into domestic and commercial premises, and this change of context was accompanied by developments in style and application as artists and craftsmen experimented with the medium.

Art Nouveau in the late nineteenth century introduced more curved lines into stained glass work. At this time the French dealer Samuel Bing opened a shop called 'L'Art Nouveau'. He encouraged a number of modern artists, among them the then unknown American, Louis Comfort Tiffany – a name which was to become central in the history of stained glass.

Tiffany was a jeweller's son, but instead of following in his father's footsteps he turned to art and interior decorating. By the late nineteenth century he was using glass increasingly in his interiors. He insisted on using opalescent glass to make all the varied shades in his designs and, in so doing, did away with the necessity of painting coloured glass. Purists were horrified, claiming that he was sacrificing the beauty of true translucent glass.

Although Tiffany became known for large works containing thousands of pieces of coloured glass, his name is now mostly identified with the Tiffany lamp. The Tiffany lampshade is made up of a great many small pieces of glass formed over a mould. The pieces of glass are so numerous and small that came cannot be used, and copper-foil is used instead.

Copper-foil is now used not only for the complicated Tiffany lampshade but for other three-dimensional objects, such as boxes and terrariums, as well as for panels and suncatchers.

A mirror-backed terrarium

MATERIALS

Mirror glass or mirror tile 25.5cm (10in) square

Clear glass 30cm (12in) square, 3mm (⅛ inch) thick

Coloured glass (optional) for roof and front. Clear glass may be used 30cm (12in) square, 3mm (⅛inch) thick

6mm (¼inch) Copper foil

Solder (about 5 sticks)

Flux

Patina (if desired)

Terrariums originated in England at the end of the nineteenth century, when many tropical plants were imported from the colonies. To prevent the delicate plants from dying during long sea journeys, little glass houses – or terrariums – were built to protect them. They are one of the easiest and most rewarding objects to make in stained glass.

The use of mirror glass in any stained glass construction gives the illusion of yet another dimension. The simplest and most rewarding form is in the use of a mirror at the back of a terrarium. With half the work and half the materials you can give the appearance of doubling its size - and that of the plants you put inside it, too.

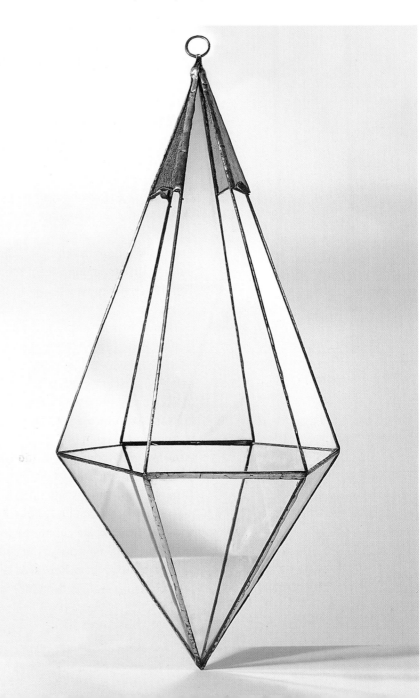

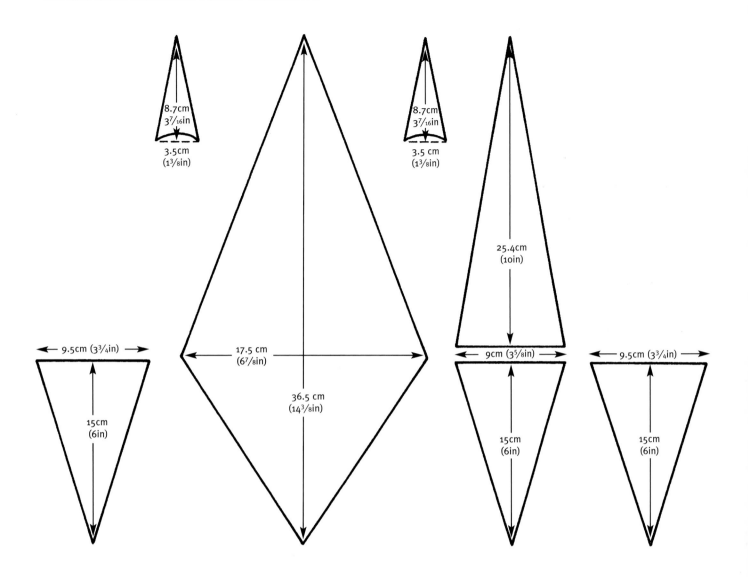

METHOD

1 Enlarge pattern to correct size (see diagram). Draw it on fairly stiff paper for durability. Cut out all pieces of glass.

2 Copper foil and tin all the edges.

3 Tape three long sides round outside of base with masking tape. Spot and seam solder the inside at base and sides. Seam and bead solder the outside. Check that construction is waterproof. If not, add more solder.

4 With masking tape attach the four roof parts. Seam and bead solder. It is not necessary to solder these joins on the inside.

5 Add small triangles of glass in top front corners to make terrarium more decorative (optional).

6 Add patina. Wash terrarium and fill with your favourite plants.

The pieces of glass cut ready for the project

Tinning: brushing flux on to the foiled edges (see page 17)

Soldering the foil to complete the tinning process

Spot soldering a seam, with a block of wood as support

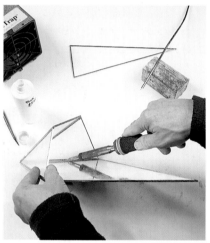

Seam soldering inside the terrarium

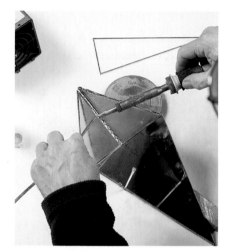

Running blobs of solder along a fluxed outer seam to create a bead solder

TO MAKE A HOOK FOR A HANGING TERRARIUM

You may be able to find a ready-made hook for hanging your terrarium but, if not, one is easily made from a length of copper wire (see photograph and further instructions on page 109). Run a length of wire, roughly 150mm (6in), round the pencil a few times leaving two ends about 25mm (1in) long. Slide the wire off the pencil, twist the two ends together and solder them to the top of the terrarium.

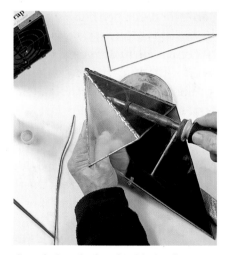

Completing the bead soldering by running the soldering iron along the blobs

A hexagonal terrarium

The hexagon is a very easy shape to use as the base for a number of projects. This design is particularly easy: you need only cut in straight lines and the measurements of the smaller sides are such that any slight errors in cutting can be adjusted when you come to the assembly and soldering stages.

With careful cutting the whole terrarium can be made from 30 x 30cm (12 x 12in) of clear glass.

METHOD

1 Draw the design onto a fairly firm piece of paper.

2 Study the suggested layout and place your design under the glass. Cut glass, remembering that glass cannot be cut 'out of' a piece of glass as a pattern piece might be from fabric – the cutting line goes right across the glass. Use a ruler to help you to keep your lines straight: if you can stick a strip of rubber on one surface of ruler, this will stop it sliding on the glass.

3 The terrarium looks quite good without a finial. If you do not want to add a finial to the roof of your terrarium leave the roof pieces intact: if you do want a finial snap off about 3mm (⅛in) from the points of your roof pieces using a pair of pliers.

4 Foil all pieces of glass (see page 16).

5 Tin all foiled pieces (see page 17).

TO ASSEMBLE

6 Place the three longest sides on top of the base leaving a space between each. Flux and then spot solder each piece in place by applying a couple of blobs of solder at the base (on the outside) of each piece – just sufficient to keep it in place. Put the smaller side pieces between the tall uprights and spot solder in position.

At this stage the slight difference in the sizes of the smaller side pieces (if your cutting has not been too accurate) might prove useful. Juggle the pieces around until you find the most acceptable fit. All the spot soldering can be done with the terrarium in an upright position.

7 After you have spot soldered the six sides to the base, turn the terrarium on its side. Apply flux to each join and run the hot soldering iron from one

MATERIALS

30 x 30cm (12 x 12in) clear glass 3mm (⅛in) thick

15 x 15cm (6 x 6in) coloured glass 3mm (⅛in) thick for roof (see diagram)

1 roll copper foil 5mm (³/₁₆in) wide (one roll will make several terrariums)

Sticks of solder

Water-soluble flux

Patina (optional) to darken or give copper finish to foil on completed terrarium

Finial (decorative roof ornament) (optional)

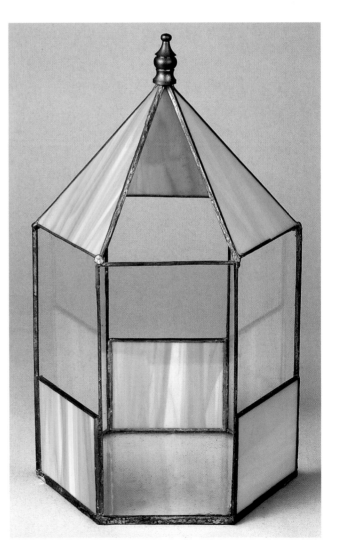

TERRARIUM CUTTING PLAN

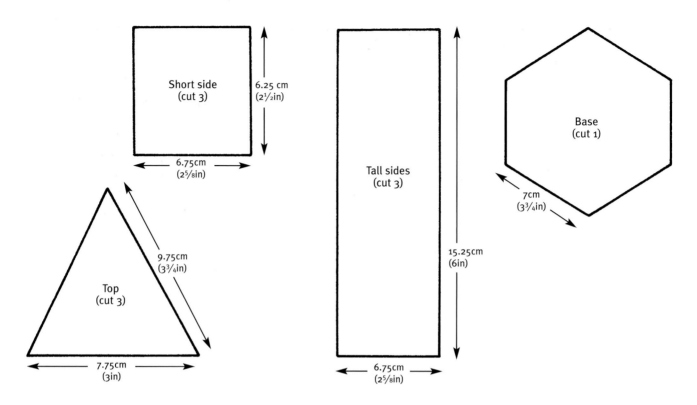

Short side
(cut 3)

6.25 cm
(2½in)

6.75cm
(2⅝in)

Top
(cut 3)

9.75cm
(3¾in)

7.75cm
(3in)

Tall sides
(cut 3)

15.25cm
(6in)

6.75cm
(2⅝in)

Base
(cut 1)

7cm
(3¾in)

CUTTING ORDER FROM A 30CM (12IN) SQUARE OF GLASS

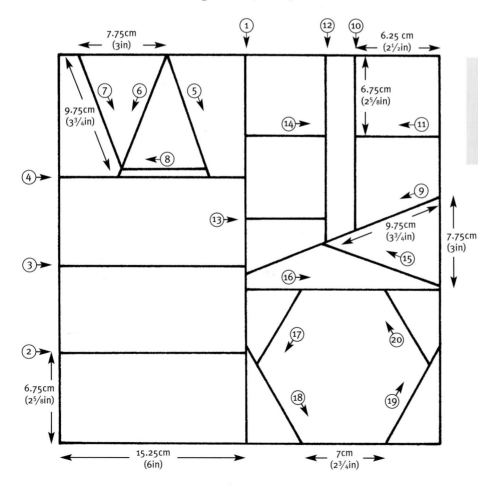

7.75cm
(3in)

9.75cm
(3¾in)

6.25 cm
(2½in)

6.75cm
(2⅝in)

9.75cm
(3¾in)

7.75cm
(3in)

6.75cm
(2⅝in)

15.25cm
(6in)

7cm
(2¾in)

HELPFUL HINT

For a very easy way to enlarge or reduce the size of a hexagon, see Hints on Calculations (page 114).

blob of solder to the next, thus forming a soldered seam. Add more solder if the seam is not fully covered. Remember that the seam you are soldering must be in a horizontal position, and wipe your soldering iron frequently on a wet rag while you are working, to keep it clean.

8 Solder all the seams on the inside, remembering to flux. Pour water in to test for any leaks. Add more solder if necessary.

TO ASSEMBLE THE ROOF
9 In order for the triangles to sit above the short sides, place each triangular piece so that its base is suspended between the corners on top of two long sides.

10 Spot solder each one in place. Finally, if you have decided not to add a finial and have left the triangular roof pieces intact – without snapping a piece off the top – solder the top points neatly together.

TO APPLY THE FINIAL
11 If you have decided to add a finial, however, apply flux to the roof of your terrarium where the three triangles meet (these should not be pointed – 3mm [⅛in] should have been cut off).

12 Scrape the surface off the finial with a sharp knife where it will touch your terrarium and apply flux. The surface has to be scraped off the brass finial to expose the surface underneath, because brass is difficult to solder.

If it is possible to borrow another pair of hands, it would be useful at this stage.

13 With a clothes peg, hold the finial in position on the top of the terrarium. Flux and solder, and continue to do both, turning the terrarium slowly until the finial feels secure.

14 Once it feels fairly secure, hold the terrarium upside down. Flux and fill the finial with solder.

15 For a good finish, apply some black or copper patina with a soft cloth. Wash the terrarium in washing-up solution, rinse well with clear water and plant up with small ivy plants.

HELPFUL HINT
I have found that in the construction of three-dimensional copper-foiled items, the final strength of the object is the same whether the sides are attached to the outside of the base or on the top of the base. As far as appearance is concerned, however, the object looks slightly neater when the sides are attached to the outside.

A little glass house for ornaments

MATERIALS

46 x 46cm (18 x 18in) clear window glass 3mm (⅛in) thick

46 x 46cm (18 x 18in) coloured glass 3mm (⅛in) thick

As a slight variation on the terrarium theme, I thought it would be rather charming to make a glass house to hold small ornaments.

METHOD

1 For the main house, from clear glass, cut:
   2 pieces 7 x 16cm (2¾ x 6¼in) for the lower parts of the back
   1 piece 11 x 16cm (4¼ x 6¼in) for the top part of the back
   3 pieces 8 x 16cm (3¼ x 6¼in) to form the base and two shelves
   4 pieces 8 x 7cm (3¼ x 2¾in) for the lower sides
   2 pieces 8 x 11 x 6.5 x 9cm (3¼ x 4¼ x 2½ x 3½in) for the top sides (see diagram)

2 From the coloured glass, cut:
   1 piece 16 x 9.5cm (6¼ x 3¾in) to form the roof

3 For the annexe, from clear glass, cut:
   2 pieces 8 x 7cm (3¼ x 2¾ in) as the lower sides which will adjoin the main house at the back and front
   2 pieces 8 x 8cm (3¼ x 3¼in) for the two floors
   2 pieces 9 x 11 x 8 x 6.5cm (3½ x 4¼ x 3¼ x 2½in) for the upper sides (see diagram)

4 From the coloured glass cut:
1 piece 9 x 8cm (3½ x 3¼in) for the roof

5 Foil and tin all pieces. Tack solder and seam solder for the main house the base, back and two sides – three times for the ground, first and top floors.

6 You now have three separate open-fronted roofless units. Stand these units on top of each other and solder them together, spot soldering first and then seam soldering – remembering to keep the seam horizontal.

7 Solder on the coloured roof. It will protrude slightly over the front.

8 To assemble the side annexe: join the two lower sides to the base and the two top sides to the first-floor base. Remember that these units have no backs.

9 To attach the annexe to the side of the house, with an opening to the side: solder it to the main building at front and back and underneath. If you can, it is best to solder inside but it is not essential here as this construction, unlike the terrarium, need not be watertight and will carry no heavy weights.

10 Finally: solder on the annexe roof.

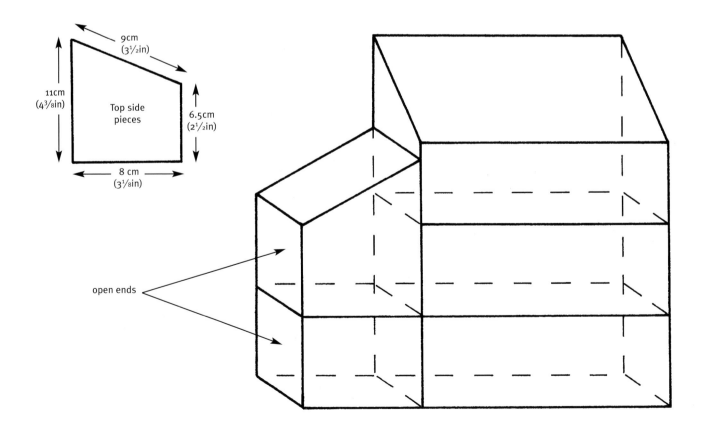

A small vase

MATERIALS

30 x 30cm (12 x 12in) coloured glass

Copper foil 5mm (³⁄₁₆in) wide

Flux and solder

Here I have chosen a small hexagon base, as used to build the terrarium on page 23, to create a vase. So simple and so effective! Using the specified quantities, you should have sufficient glass left over to make a smaller single-bud vase.

METHOD

1 Cut six pieces coloured glass 3 x 17.5cm (1¼ x 7in) for the sides.

2 Foil and tin.

3 Spot and solder together the six sides, taking care to keep the hexagonal shape accurate at the top and bottom of vase.

4 Stand your soldered tube on paper and trace around it.

5 Cut glass to this shape for your base. Foil and tin.

6 Solder tube to base.

A multicoloured bowl

Made from as many different colours as are deemed compatible, this bowl is most colourful and attractive – just one of many decorative, interesting and functional objects which can be made with stained glass.

METHOD

1 Using the diagram, cut your base in mirror glass. Cut sides and corner pieces in as many different colours as you wish.

2 Foil and tin all your edges (see page 17).

3 Spot solder six straight sides to outside of base so that they are only just attached and can be tilted later to the desired angle.

4 Fit your six corner pieces snugly between the side pieces and hold them in place with masking tape.

5 Spot solder and then bead solder all the joins both inside and outside.

6 Apply antique or copper patina with a soft cloth.

7 Wash the bowl in mild washing-up solution and polish with soft cloth.

MATERIALS

Small pieces of coloured glass (see diagram)

11 x 11cm (approx 4½ x 4½in) mirror glass

Copper foil, flux, solder, patina

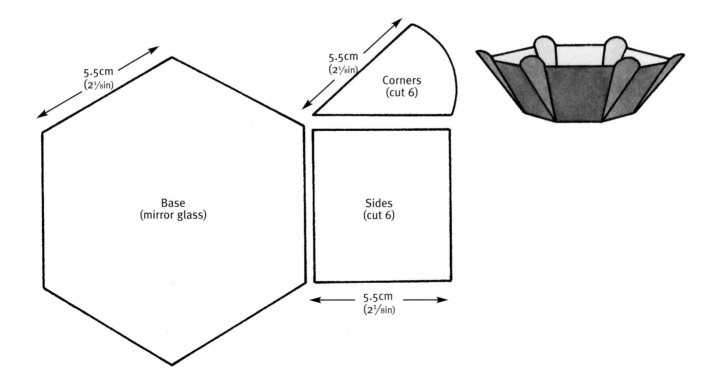

5.5cm (2⅛in)

Base (mirror glass)

5.5cm (2⅛in)

Corners (cut 6)

Sides (cut 6)

5.5cm (2⅛in)

A night-light holder

MATERIALS

Small pieces of coloured glass (mirror glass optional)

Copper-foil

Solder, flux, patina

The beauty of a stained glass night-light holder can be enhanced if you can construct it so that it is fairly narrow at the top. However, this type of construction makes inserting the night-light from the top extremely difficult. With this in mind, I have designed a holder where the night-light can be inserted and lit at the base.

It is advisable to stand the night-light on a small metal dish in the finished holder. In this way, when the night-light burns down to the bottom, the base will be protected from the heat which might otherwise crack the glass. It also helps to contain the wax and makes cleaning the holder much easier.

METHOD

1 Cut all the pieces as shown in the diagram: the base can be made from either mirror glass or coloured cathedral glass, whichever you prefer. Cut one of the top long side pieces about 2 mm (¹⁄₁₆ in) wider than the other five at the base. This is because it will have to span an 'open space' in your construction.

2 Copper-foil and tin all edges (see page 17).

3 Spot solder and solder five side pieces to the outside of the base. The remaining 'open space' is where the night-light will be inserted in the finished holder.

4 Spot solder all the taller triangular side pieces on to the sides. Remember to place the slightly larger-based piece over the gap left for inserting the night-light (see diagram).

5 Tilt all these pointed sides slightly until the smaller triangles fit snugly in between. Spot solder these smaller pieces into place.

6 When you are satisfied with your spot-soldered construction, seam solder and bead solder (see earlier projects for details on soldering). You will not be able to solder on the inside with this

construction. However, as the holder will not have to contain water, this is not necessary.

7 Apply patina.

8 Wash in mild detergent and polish with soft cloth.

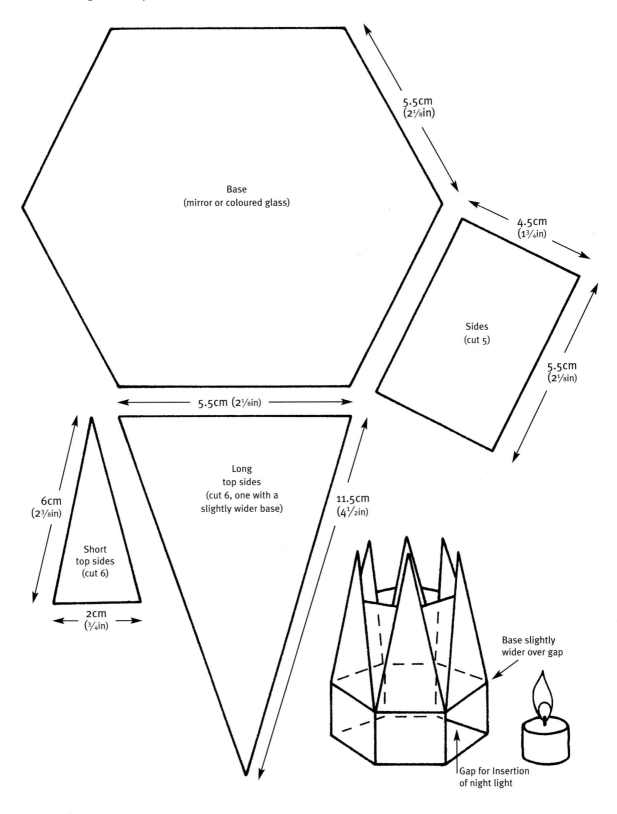

5.5cm
(2⅛in)

Base
(mirror or coloured glass)

4.5cm
(1¾in)

Sides
(cut 5)

5.5cm
(2⅛in)

5.5cm (2⅛in)

Long
top sides
(cut 6, one with a
slightly wider base)

11.5cm
(4½in)

6cm
(2⅜in)

Short
top sides
(cut 6)

2cm
(¾in)

Base slightly
wider over gap

Gap for Insertion
of night light

A simple box

MATERIALS

Oddments of glass

Copper-foil

Solder, flux, patina

This little box can use up any small pieces of glass which you may have left over from other projects. For simplicity's sake I have used different colours on the lid only, but you could, of course, 'mix and match' on the sides and ends, too.

METHOD

1 For the base, from mirror glass, cut:
   1 piece 13 x 8cm (5¼ x 3½in)

2 For the two sides, from plain glass cut:
   2 pieces 13 x 4cm (5¼ x 1¾in)

3 For the ends cut:
   2 pieces 8 x 4cm (3½x 1¾in)

4 For the lid cut pieces to fit, in this case:
   1 piece of plain glass 13 x 2.5 x 1.5cm (5¼ x 1 x ⅝in)
   1 piece of plain glass 13 x 3.5 x 1.5 cm (5¼ x 1⅜ x ⅝in)
   1 piece of coloured glass 13 x 4 x 3cm (5¼ x 1¾ x 1⅛in) for the centre band

5 Solder together the pieces of the lid by placing them flat on bench and bead soldering the seams. Put aside.

6 Assemble box as for the terrarium.

7 Attach the lid of the box with a hinge (see page 108)

8 Apply black patina and polish to all seams. Clean as for terrariums. Stick felt to base to protect furniture.

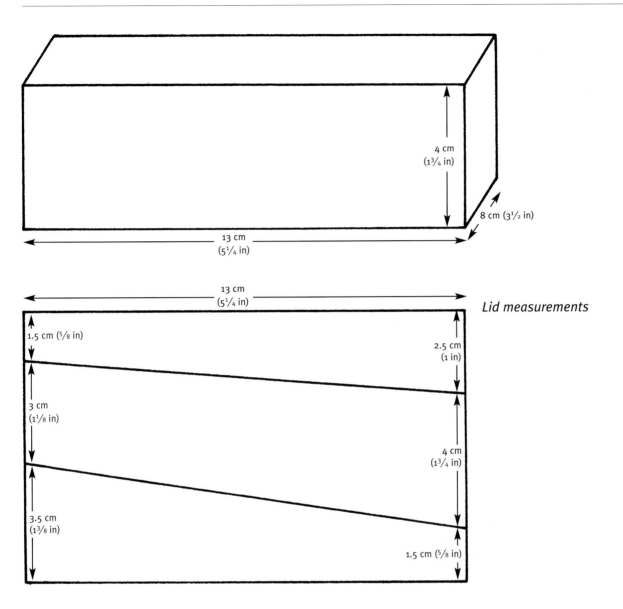

Lid measurements

OTHER DESIGN SUGGESTIONS FOR THE LID

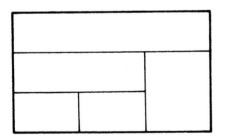
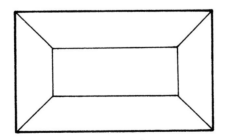

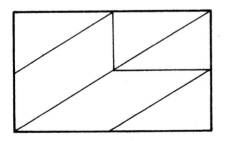
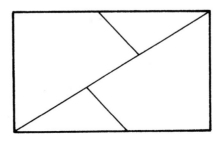

TANGRAMS

Although tangrams are still not widely recognized, it was four thousand years ago that the legendary Chinaman Tan first cut a square into the seven pieces shown in my diagram (facing page).

It soon became apparent that numerous designs could be made from just these seven pieces. In fact, books have been written illustrating more than three hundred different tangram designs. Using two or more tangrams, it is possible to make pictures depicting two or more figures and animals - and, of course, to incorporate several colours.

I realized the potential of the tangram in connection with stained glass as soon as I saw that all the lines were straight. Not a single curve to cut – what absolute bliss for the beginner tackling the cutting of glass for the first time. And, of course, there is the added bonus that not a scrap of glass is wasted.

This suncatcher is just one of the designs that resulted from my experiments. Once you know how to assemble a suncatcher you will be able to create any number of designs with tangrams.

METHOD

1 Place the tangram template under your glass. Make your first cut a diagonal line from corner to corner. Proceed with all the small cuts in the way you find easiest.

2 Foil all pieces and tin all foiled glass (see page 17).

3 Lay out the pieces in the design you have chosen on a good flat surface .

4 Spot solder, seam solder and bead solder.

5 Cut a piece of wire approximately 10mm (³⁄₈in) long. Shape it into a U and, remembering to flux first, solder the ends along the edge of the tangram.

6 Hang with nylon fishing thread.

MATERIALS

11 x 11cm (4½ x 4½in) coloured glass – or any size of square you prefer

Copper foil

Solder

Flux

Wire to make a hook on which to hang the finished suncatcher (thick fuse wire, or a piece of a paper clip, is quite acceptable for small suncatchers)

CUTTING ORDER

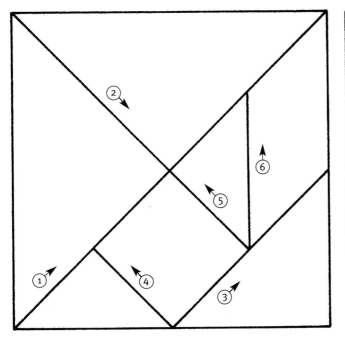

THE SEPARATE PIECES

Suncatchers from small pieces of glass

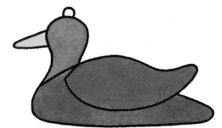

You will be astonished at how much cullet (small pieces of glass) seems to accumulate – even after a few projects. The best way to store the cullet is in plastic ice-cream containers, or something similar. If possible, have a box for each colour.

There are several ways in which to use up these small pieces of glass: making suncatchers is one. Not only fun to make, these small colourful mobiles send out rays of different colours as they hang on windows, twisting and twirling in the breeze.

I have made several suncatchers from my cullet boxes. Some have required no glass cutting at all – the girl smelling a flower, for example (see illustration). After all, it doesn't matter with a suncatcher what size any part of it is, so there is no need for any precision in design.

METHOD

1 Either create your own design or enlarge the diagram and use one of these figures as a template.

2 Position your pieces of glass according to your chosen design.

3 Copper foil and tin each piece.

4 Replace foiled pieces on to design. Keep in place with small pieces of masking tape.

5 Flux and spot solder.

6 Run solder along the joins. With small items like these you will not need to add any more solder – use that already on your work where you have spot soldered. (If you are making the little girl smelling the flower, straighten out a paper clip for the flower's stem and to support the flower.)

7 Make a small hanging hook, either from thin tinned copper wire or a paper clip. Bend the wire in half and twist it to make a loop. Flatten out the ends along your mobile, and solder.

8 Hang up with fishing nylon.

Bird and Fish mirror

A mirror to brighten up your bathroom. The finished mirror measures 30 x 45cm (12 x 18in). As it will be hanging against a wall, it is best to use opalescent glass.

METHOD

1 Enlarge diagram to the correct size to create your templates. My list of materials is for a 30 x 45cm (12 x 18in) mirror, but you can make your mirror bigger or smaller if you prefer. Make two copies.

2 Stick the second copy on to thin cardboard (cereal boxes are very good for this) and cut out the design from the cardboard. These pieces will be used as your templates.

3 Using templates on top of your glass, cut out all the coloured pieces. Do not cut out your mirror glass at this stage.

4 Copper foil and tin all coloured pieces.

MATERIALS

30 x 45cm (12 x 18in) mirror glass

30 x 45cm (12 x 18in) mirror backing to protect the back of mirror from damp

Clear nail varnish to protect mirror back before fluxing

15 x 45cm (6 x 18in) dark green opalescent glass

15 x 20cm (6 x 8in) light blue opalescent glass

Light green, light and dark blue, orange red, light and dark amber offcuts

5mm ($^{7}/_{32}$in) copper foil

Solder (two sticks should be adequate)

Flux

Black patina

4 wall clips

5 Spot solder and seam solder according to your pattern.

6 Place the coloured glass frame on a piece of cardboard and draw around the inside. Cut out this template.

7 Place this template on top of your mirror glass and, making all cuts on the front of the mirror, cut out the required shape. When you get to a curved part (the clouds, for example), lift off the cutter and cut the curve going right to the edge of the mirror in each direction.

8 Paint all around the edge of the back of mirror, where you are going to apply flux, with clear nail varnish. This varnish rim should be about 10mm (⅜in) wide: it will stop the flux 'eating' into the silver backing of the mirror.

Enlarge your diagram to the correct size, with a colour guide

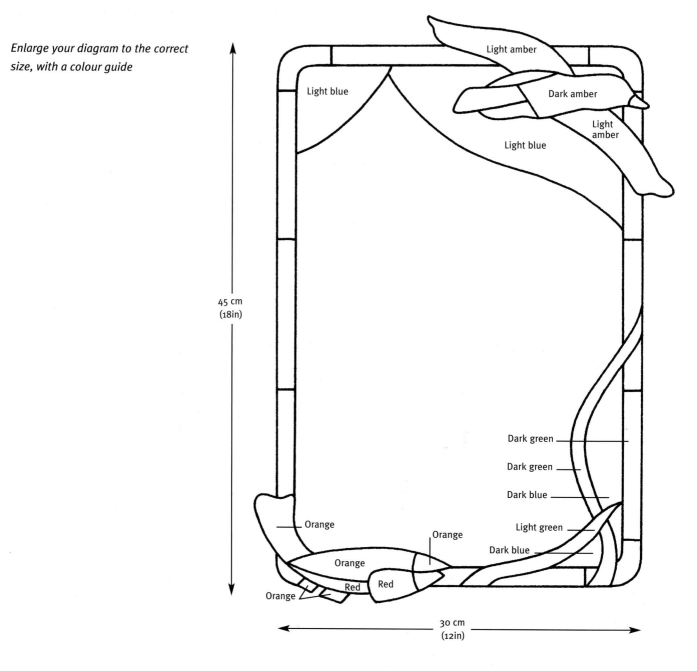

45 cm
(18in)

Light amber

Light blue

Dark amber

Light amber

Light blue

Dark green

Dark green

Dark blue

Light green

Dark blue

Orange

Orange

Orange

Red

Red

Orange

30 cm
(12in)

11 Foil the edge of the mirror and place into its opalescent glass 'frame'.

12 Spot and seam solder the mirror into the 'frame'. Bead solder all the front seams.

13 Turn mirror over and seam solder the back.

14 Apply mirror backing to protect mirror from damp. Secure wall clips on the wall. Placing the mirror in position, slide the clips in place over edge of the mirror.

Alternatively, reverse the mirror and place 16-gauge copper wire across the back, about a third of the way down. Solder it to the inner side of he border and carry the wire down to a join, soldering all the way along (see diagram). In this way you can hang the mirror with a decorative chain.

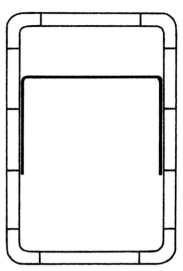

Soldering copper wire to the back of the mirror for hanging

Bordered mirror with tulip design

A n easier bordered mirror using opalescent glass: the mirror glass is cut in only one place and even that is relatively straightforward. The diagram illustrates both the three-tulip motif used in the featured finished mirror and a variation on it – the choice is yours.

Follow instructions as for the Bird and Fish mirror. I used yet another hanging method for this mirror, attaching a chain to the back and hanging it on a pair of picture hooks.

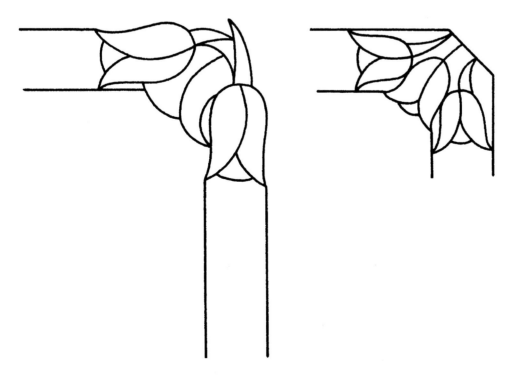

A Tiffany panel lampshade

MATERIALS

91 x 91cm (36 x 36in) opalescent glass
3mm(⅛in) thick (I used 300 x 300mm
[12 x 12in] each of red, green and grey)

Small amount of 5mm (⁷⁄₃₂in) copper foil

Thin cardboard for templates

Vase cap and finial

Wooden triangle

HELPFUL HINT

You should always use a wooden
triangle to make panel-shaped
shades. It is a good idea
gradually to build up a collection
of these triangular frames in
different sizes.

True Tiffany lampshades are made with many small pieces of
opalescent and/or iridescent glass – sometimes as many as five or
six hundred. This sounds an alarming number of pieces, but it is
surprising how quickly the lamp can be built. Tiffany shades are
generally one of three basic shapes: cone shaped – similar, as the
name suggests, to an outspread ice-cream cone; panel-shaped – made
up of a series of panels; and dome-shaped – similar to the dome of
St Paul's Cathedral, London.

The panel shape is the easiest to make, as all the panels can be
made and assembled flat. The cone shape is a little more difficult to
make and must be assembled over a suitable mould. The dome
shape is also formed entirely over a mould. It is the hardest type to
make because your curves go in all directions – up and down and
sideways.

Panel shades can be made using only the copper-foil technique. For
this design, your eight panels should be identically angled.

TO MAKE THE WOODEN TRIANGLE

On a piece of wood approx. 16 x 27cm (approx. 6 x 11in) nail three
wooden strips in a triangle that matches exactly the shape of your panel
design. This triangle will help you keep all your panels exactly the same
size and shape.

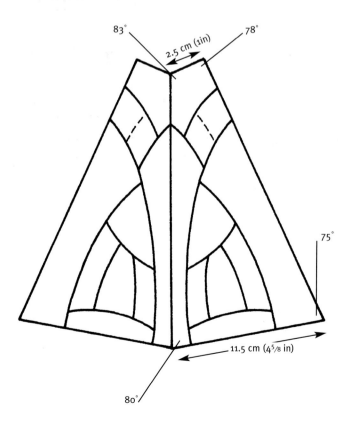

METHOD

1 Trace the design on to thin cardboard with a felt-tipped pen.

2 To make your templates, cut out each piece of the pattern inside the felt-pen line: this makes allowance for the copper-foiled edges in your construction.

3 This lampshade is made up of eight panels. Place the template on your glass, draw around it and cut four identical pieces. Turn the template over, draw around the template and cut out four more pieces of glass.

4 Copper foil and tin each piece.

5 Place your tinned pieces into your wooden triangle following the design. Spot seam and bead solder. Remember to reverse four panels. I have left a few pieces of glass out of my shade at the top for added ventilation and also to create a more unusual design (see photo). Seam solder the second side.

6 Lay the eight pieces in a circle on a flat surface and lightly join the panels with masking tape at about 50mm (2in) from the top and the same distance from the base of the shade. Stand it up against a bottle or something similar. You will need to enlist a second pair of hands at this stage.

7 Spot solder at the top of the shade and at each junction between sections. Spot solder the sides as near to the base as possible. Roughly seam solder the full length of the side joins while the lamp is in this upright position, by letting solder run down from the top to the base.

8 As soon as the shade feels fairly secure, turn it onto its side, supporting it with something soft. Seam and bead solder each side.

9 Attach the vase cap (see page 110). Attach the harp to the stand, place the shade on the harp and secure with a finial.

10 Apply patina. Wash and polish.

HELPFUL HINT

When securing foiled pieces of glass in position with masking tape, protect your foiled edges with pieces of paper or the tape will pull the foil from the glass when it is removed.

Bouquet of Flowers lampshade

MATERIALS

Mould (I would recommend a full-form mould and not a sectional one)

2 copies of the design

Pritt stick or something similar (not glue)

8cm (3¼in) vase cap

Harp and finial

46 x 46cm (18 x 18in) opalescent glass for the main background pieces

30 x 30cm (12 x 12in) each of opalescent red, blue and pink glass for the flowers

30 x 30cm (12 x 12in) opalescent green glass for the leaves

Flux and solder

1 roll 5mm (⁷⁄₃₂in) copper-foil. If you use a narrower foil it will cause weaknesses in your finished shade should your foiling be at all uneven, while wider foil will make your joins appear clumsy.

A traditional Tiffany lampshade (finished lamp 30 cm [12in] diameter) using a mould. It is possible to make a Tiffany lampshade with many fewer pieces than the originals: this 'bouquet of flowers' shade is just one example.

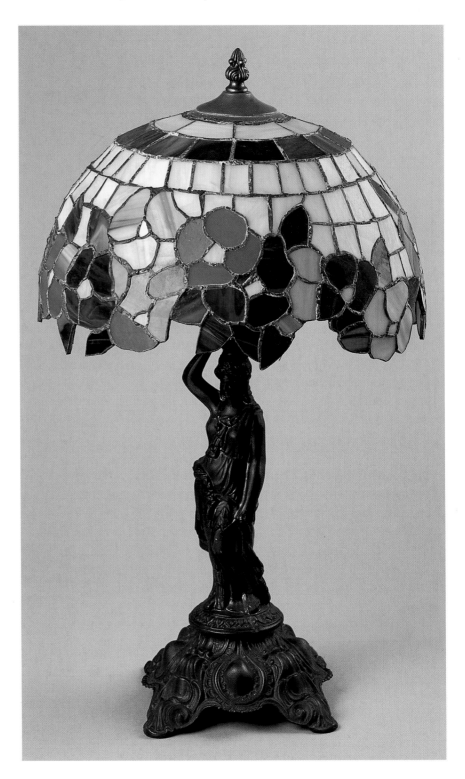

METHOD

1 Trace one copy of your grid and another of your flower design on to greaseproof paper or paper of similar thickness. These tracings will be attached to the mould. Make a second tracing, to be cut up and used as templates, on thicker paper or thin cardboard (cereal boxes are good).

2 Attach your vase cap to your mould. Place the cap centrally over the hole at the top of your mould. (If your mould has no hole, I would advise that you make one, because it makes constructing the lamp much easier, but take care to have it absolutely in the centre.) Put your finial on the vase cap. Screw a 50mm (2in) length of threaded rod through the mould, vase cap and into the finial and secure it underneath with a nut.

3 Apply the greaseproof-paper tracing of the main grid at the top of mould to abut the edge of the vase cap (see diagram). Follow the instructions on the diagram.

4 Stick your flower design in position at bottom of the mould at whatever depth you want it. Remember that it has to hide the electric light bulb and fittings, so do not make it too shallow. Attach your designs to the mould with stick rather than permanent glue because you will want to remove the design so that you can re-use the mould.

5 Check that your completed design (as stuck on your mould) is the same as that traced onto your cardboard.

HELPFUL HINT

When making a lampshade with a non-symmetrical design, it is virtually impossible to keep strictly to the pattern in the final stages of assembly. You will have to adjust the pattern as you work. No one will notice, after all, whether two leaves or flower petals are exactly the same size as the previous flower repeat. However accurately you seem to cut your glass, this adjustment seems inevitable.

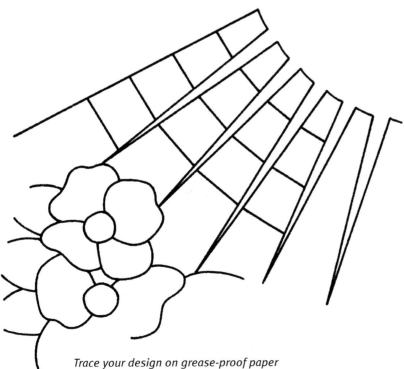

Trace your design on grease-proof paper so that it fits snugly around the vase cap

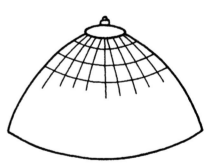

Attach traced grid to mould with Pritt stick

Attach flower design to mould

Tin the pieces first, and the solder will flow more freely.

BEGIN THE CONSTRUCTION OF YOUR SHADE FROM THE TOP

6 Cut out your templates and your glass for the first row of pieces, which will abut your vase cap.

7 Copper foil and tin each piece. It might seem tedious and unnecessary to tin these small pieces, but it really is worthwhile. When you are assembling them the solder will flow much more freely between tinned pieces than it would untinned pieces. Moreover, this will give more strength to your finished shade.

8 Using a glue stick, secure the first row of glass around your mould as close to your vase cap as possible. Add masking tape at the bottom edges of the glass and onto the mould if the Pritt does not hold the glass securely. If your mould is made of polystyrene, use large-headed pins to hold your glass pieces in place.

9 Spot solder and seam solder all the glass pieces together. You now have a soldered 'collar' at the top of your mould.

10 Attach vase cap and collar (see page 110). This forms a very secure foundation on which to continue to build your shade.

11 Continue assembling your shade working round and round the mould. Spot and seam solder each row as you proceed.

12 Bead solder all seams. Remove the shade from the mould and solder all inside seams. Rest the upside-down shade on a soft support while you do this (newspaper shavings are quite good).

14 Finally, add black patina and wash in washing-up solution. Attach the harp to the stand of your choice. Put the shade on the harp and secure it with the finial.

Grapes and Leaves lampshade

Y ou can make a pleasing lampshade using glass globs (see page 5) as the focal point of your design. I have drawn a flat cartoon of my lampshade of grapes and leaves. It is virtually impossible to design an accurate cartoon when using nuggets because they vary considerably in size and shape.

This lampshade (for a lamp with 32.5cm [13in] diameter base) is both interesting to look at when it is unlit and throws a delightful coloured pattern over its surroundings when lit.

MATERIALS

32.5mm (13in) mould

96 red globs

61 x 61cm (24 x 24in) light green opalescent glass

61 x 61cm (24 x 24in) mid-green streaked glass

61 x 61cm (24 x 24in) dark green opalescent glass

Small piece of amber cathedral glass for stalks

Small piece of light blue cathedral glass for sky between leaves

7.5cm (3in) vase cap

5mm (⁷⁄₃₂in) copper-foil (as for bouquet lampshade above)

METHOD

1 Make up your bunches of grapes: 9 bunches of 6 grapes, 12 bunches of 3 grapes and 3 bunches of 2 grapes. Foil each glob with 4mm ($^5/_{32}$in) copper foil, tin and assemble. You will have quite a lot of solder between the globs, but this adds to the finished design.

2 Attach the vase cap to the top of the mould with a threaded rod and two nuts.

3 Stick white paper over your mould in tapered strips starting at the edge of the vase cap and finishing at the base of the mould (using a glue stick).

4 Draw the position of the bunches of grapes on this paper. Number the globs on your corresponding drawings. Draw in the remainder of the design between the grapes.

5 Remove the design from the mould and make a copy by tracing it.

6 Reposition your original drawing on your mould.

7 Using your traced copy, cut out templates for each piece of your design using thin cardboard.

8 Continue building up your lampshade as for the 'Bouquet of Flowers' lampshade (page 42).

Small Tiffany lampshade made on a home-found mould

It is astonishing how many household items make suitable moulds. If you are going to finish your shade with a vase cap you must use a mould which is rounded at the bottom (this will be the top of your shade). Wok lids and salad bowls are good in this respect, but both these objects will prove rather shallow used as a mould. If you do use either of these, you will have to balance your mould on a block of wood or something similar (the height you require for your completed shade), and then you will have to complete your shade working freehand – that is, without a support for your mould.

Experimenting is fun. Here I have made an open-topped lampshade using a plastic 1kg (2lb) pudding basin as my mould. It is worth remembering that if you use a plastic basin as a mould you can draw your design directly onto it with pencil (see illustration), because it can be removed when you have finished your shade.

MATERIALS

Plastic pudding basin

46 x 46cm (18 x 18in) opalescent or iridised glass for the background

Small piece of coloured opalescent glass 3mm (⅛in) thick for flowers

5mm (⁷⁄₃₂in) copper foil

Flux and solder

Patina (if desired)

2 copies of the design

METHOD

Follow the assembly instructions given for the traditional 'Bouquet of Flowers' shade (page 42), omitting all the instructions about attaching a vase cap. The result will be very pleasing.

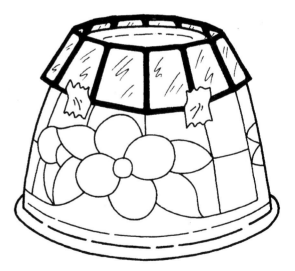

Serviceable lampshade moulds are all about us in the home

THE APPLIQUÉ TECHNIQUE

Appliqué is the term used to describe the technique in which small pieces of coloured glass are stuck onto a base of clear glass to form the design. With modern glues it is an extremely easy technique, so I hope you will be tempted to experiment.

You should use either epoxy resin or glass bond. If you are working on a large piece you should use epoxy resin. It is sold in two parts: resin and hardener. Make sure you are working in a well-ventilated room, mix the two parts thoroughly before using and do not mix more than you can apply in half an hour at one time. You must also apply the resin in a very thin layer: thick layers applied to different types of glass cause stresses and eventually crack the glass.

For small panels I favour glass bond because it is easy to apply. It does have one drawback, however – it relies on strong daylight to make fast the bonding. Because it does not depend on daylight for its adhesion, clear glue is even easier to use, and although some clear glues do leave a slight film on the glass, this will not matter if you are working with opalescent glass.

With the appliqué technique you can radically alter the design by the amount of grouting you have between the pieces of glass. Whereas with came or copper-foil the lines between the pieces of glass are of uniform thickness throughout, the opaque patches caused by the grouting in appliqué can vary from thin lines to very large areas. This should be taken into account when deciding a pattern.

A candle holder in appliqué

MATERIALS

4 pieces window glass 12.5 x 17.5cm (5 x 7in); 4mm ($^5/_{32}$in) thick for sides

13 x 13cm (5$^1/_8$ x 5$^1/_8$in) window glass; 4mm ($^5/_{32}$in) thick for base

Lots of pieces of coloured glass (cullet)

Glass bond (obtainable in hardware shops)

Tile grouting

Small amounts of watercolour or poster paint to colour grout

METHOD

1 Copper-foil and tin all your cut pieces of window glass.

2 Arrange your coloured pieces of glass in the desired pattern on a plain piece of paper. (I made two sides with a mixture of orange, red, yellow and pink pieces of glass, and the two other sides I made with various shades of green and blue.)

3 Transfer the pieces one by one onto your glass and stick them down with glass bond. You only need a very small amount of glass bond.

4 When all pieces are in place, balance the panel on a milk bottle to let the daylight get underneath. This is necessary because glass bond's rapid adhesive action is triggered by ultraviolet rays (present in natural daylight). To allow the light to go underneath will counteract the fact that the coloured glass will be slowing down the bonding process. The pieces of glass thus exposed to daylight will bond almost immediately on a bright day.

HELPFUL HINT

It is advisable to place a small tin lid on the base to hold the candle – to collect the wax and mimimize the likelihood of the glass cracking should the candle burn down too low.

5 As soon as the glass pieces are securely, stuck on all four sides mix a small amount of tile grouting in a dish. Add watercolour or poster paint if desired. (I added red poster paint to the grouting for the red/orange side and blue poster paint for the blue/green sides.)

6 Spread the grouting between the glass with a small palette knife. Wipe off any surplus from the surface of the glass with a damp cloth and leave to dry. The pieces of glass are now securely stuck or appliquéd to your panels.

TO ASSEMBLE THE CANDLE HOLDER

7 As you did for the terrarium, place the sides on top of the base, and – with each side attached to the inside of one adjoining panel and to the outside of the other – spot solder together the sides and fix them onto the base.

8 Seam solder. Apply copper or black patina if desired.

Small hanging plaques

METHOD

1 Draw your chosen design on sturdy paper (see page 52).

2 Cut out clear glass base and place it on top of your design.

3 Decide on colours and then prepare your glass. Place pieces of coloured glass between thick layers of newspaper and hit firmly with a hammer – not too vigorously or the glass fragments will be too small to handle. For a circular plaque 180mm (7in) in diameter the pieces should not be smaller than 12.5mm (½in).

5 Put a small blob of glass bond on the clear glass and place a broken piece on top. Proceed in this way, placing one piece of glass on to the base at a time. It is a slow job but very absorbing. When your design is complete place your work in strong daylight. Because the light passes more easily through the clear glass and rather slowly through the coloured glass, place your work on top of a jam jar (or something similar) to allow the light to penetrate from underneath. If you are using epoxy resin, follow the manufacturer's instructions.

6 Allow at least 24 hours for the glass to dry completely. Then, if you have bought grouting in powder form, mix it with water. Take the amount you intend to use from your container and place it in a shallow plastic or glass dish (the lid from a coffee jar will do if your work is

MATERIALS

Clear glass at least 3mm (⅛in) thick for base

Coloured cullet

Epoxy resin or glass bond

Grouting (ordinary tile grouting is the easiest to use: you can colour it with paint)

Old palette knife or something similar to apply the grouting

Small amount of watercolour or poster paint (optional)

C came for framing

Wire to make hooks

Chain for hanging

small – 180mm [7½in] or less in diameter). Add watercolour or poster paint to tint the grout: black is generally very effective, but any colour may be used.

7   Apply grouting between all the pieces of glass using a palette knife. It will smooth over the glass, but that does not matter.

8   With a wet cloth – and before the grouting hardens too much – wipe off any surplus grouting from the glass.

9   Allow to dry for approximately 24 hours. Add hooks and a hanging chain.

DESIGNS FOR AN APPLIQUÉ HANGING PLAQUE

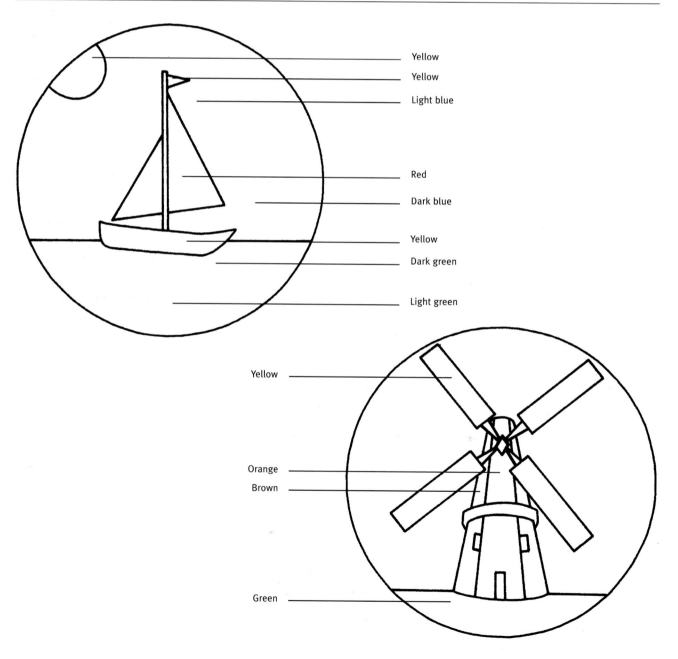

Yellow

Yellow

Light blue

Red

Dark blue

Yellow

Dark green

Light green

Yellow

Orange

Brown

Green

Cottage lamp

Making this cottage lamp using the appliqué method is great fun, and the results are startling. When it is lit, beautiful colours will flow through it, and at other times it will be an attractive ornament.

I show how to fit an electric light bulb to the lamp. You can use a night light for illumination, but this is not advisable if the lamp is to be used in a child's room.

METHOD

1 With a ruler measure 140mm (5½in) up the side of your glass jar and mark a line around it, using a chinagraph pencil or permanent ink pen.

2 Score a line over your drawn line with your cutter. Do this very slowly: if you cut at speed your cutter will shoot off the side of the jar. I find that the easiest way to make the score line is to wedge the jar against a heavy object and to rotate it slowly, keeping the cutter almost stationary.

3 After you have scored your line, place your jar first in hot and then in cold water. Do this a few times and, if you are lucky, the jar will fall into two pieces – watch your hands at this stage. If the glass does not break readily, tap it along the score line with the ball end of your cutter (both inside and outside).

MATERIALS

One large confectionary or pickled onion jar approx. 165mm (6½in) in diameter (If you use a smaller jar, remember to adjust your roof measurements)

30 x 30cm (12 x 12in) (clear or opalescent) coloured glass for the roof and chimney

Lots of pieces of coloured glass (cullet) mainly opalescent (For my red 'cottage' I used mainly red and orange opalescent glass broken into randomly shaped pieces. For the amber 'cottage' I used various shades of amber and yellow opalescent glass cut roughly into oblong and square shapes)

Clear glue or glass bond (As I was using mainly opalescent glass I used clear glue)

Small length of 5mm (⁷⁄₃₂in) copper foil for roof and top of jar if the cut glass has not been ground down

Small amount of tile grouting

Glass paint

Light-bulb holder (if lamp is to be used with electricity)

Piece of wood at least 20mm (¾in) thick on which to screw bulb holder

Night light (if not using electricity)

HELPFUL HINT

It is important that the grouting is mixed to a fairly stiff consistency, for if it is too liquid it will run under your glass pieces and spoil the look of your work.

Some people prefer to use this latter method because they find the breaking glass of the hot-and-cold water method rather too dramatic.

4 If you have access to a grinder use it to grind the cut edge of your jar until it has no sharp edges. If you have no grinder, foil and tin the cut edge of the jar.

5 (If you are going to use a light bulb.) Make a hole at the base of the jar to admit the electric wire. If you do not have a glass grinder with a hole-drilling attachment, any glass merchant will do this for you – provided that you do not go when he is busy. You could ask him to grind the top of your jar at the same time.

6 Using a chinagraph pencil or permanent ink pen, draw in windows and doors.

7 Break up oddments of glass into small pieces or cut them into square or oblong shapes. No piece of glass should be larger than 20mm (¾in) in any direction. To break the glass into irregular pieces, place it in the centre of a folded newspaper and hit it with a hammer (this is great fun) until you have numerous glass pieces of varying shapes.

8 Stick the small pieces of glass to the jar, leaving the door and window spaces clear. Then leave it for approximately 24 hours until the glass pieces are securely stuck.

9 Mix a small amount of grouting as per the manufacturer's directions. If you are colouring your grouting it should be done at this stage; just

MAKING THE COTTAGE LAMP

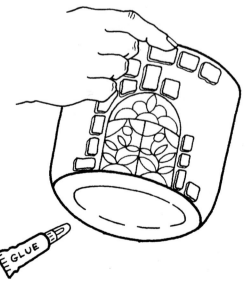

mix some watercolour or poster paint of the desired colour with the water you are using to mix the grout.

10 Apply the grouting between the glass pieces with an old palette knife. Wipe off any excess grouting from the surface of the glass with a damp cloth.

11 With glass paints, using either a small brush or the outliner from the tube, draw in the windows and doors. (I enjoyed making a 'stained glass' door on one of my lamps.) Complete the painting with colours.

TO MAKE THE ROOF AND CHIMNEY

12 Using coloured glass cut out the roof and chimney pieces as shown in the pattern. Copper foil all edges. Tin and solder together the six main pieces of the roof. Spot solder, seam solder and finish all joins with a bead solder seam.

13 Solder together the chimney pieces. Decide where you want the chimney and mark the position with a chinagraph pencil. Stick 5mm (³⁄₁₆in) copper foil over pencil lines. Flux and solder the chimney onto the copper-foil strips.

14 Place the roof on the base: it will balance quite securely.

15 (If you are using a light bulb.) Screw a light-bulb holder onto a piece of thick wood and place this onto the base: a piece of Blu-tack will keep it steady. Attach an electric wire and thread this through the hole in the base of the jar.

TRADITIONAL STAINED GLASS USING LEAD CAME

Traditional lead came technique was used for many centuries for windows in both ecclesiastical and domestic dwellings. Magnificent stained glass, dependent largely upon its colour, greatly enhanced ecclesiastical Gothic architecture for four hundred years from the twelfth century. As with all forms of art, however, people began to experiment: they were looking for methods by which to alter the appearance of the pure colours, and in the seventeenth and eighteenth centuries craftsmen began to use enamels to paint details on to the clear colours. Traditional stained glass, then, is the result of a combination of coloured glass and glass enhanced by paint.

Not welcomed at first, this new approach was eventually accepted. If you get close enough to an old stained-glass window you will see that a great percentage of it is painted (the Henry Cole wing of the Victoria and Albert Museum in London has some good examples). While some parts are made with lead, much of the black outline is painted.

As most people do not have access to a kiln, I have used pigments which require no firing to paint in the details, choosing a modern transparent paint instead – Deka, Pebeo or Vitrael. Further on in the book I describe traditional painting on glass and firing, so if you prefer the 'true' painting method please refer to Painting on Glass (page 79).

The ideal arrangement for painting on glass is to place a piece of glass on an easel and then to attach the panel on which you will be painting to the plate glass with either beeswax or Blu-tack. Alternatively you can use a light box (see How to build a light box and How to make a glass-painting easel, pages 11-12). If neither of these options is possible, however, lay your glass panel on a light-coloured surface.

Victorian-style window panel

MATERIALS

30 x 35cm (12 x 18in) plain glass

12x 14cm (5 x 7¼in) green glass for leaves

10 x 10cm (4 x 4in) red glass for outside flower

Small piece of orange glass for bud

8 x 8cm (3¼ x 3¼in) amber glass for horizontal petals

136cm (54in) C came for border

280cm (112in) H came

approx. 35 x 40cm (14 x 16in) chipboard, with raised wooden surround

In addition to the usual glass tools used for copper-foil work, you will need:

Vice for holding lead while stretching it

Nova tool, lathekin or wedge-shaped piece of wood for opening lead (a wooden doorstop will do)

Lead-cutting knife (sharp kitchen knife or Stanley-type knife)

Large Victorian houses had delightful stained-glass windows. They varied from a few modest pieces of coloured glass with plain glass surrounds, describing flowers and leaves, to more lavish colourful designs – usually above the heavy front doors. Regrettably, early in the twentieth century many Victorian residences were 'modernized', the beautiful stained glass removed and replaced with plain glass. Nowadays, however, this trend has been reversed and stained glass is once more in demand – both as authentic Victorian-style detailing in houses of the period, and to enhance and complement both existing and new buildings.

It was with this in mind that I designed a very simple pattern in the Victorian style. This finished panel measures 30 x 35cm (12 x 14in),

HELPFUL HINT

When making windows with glass which is textured on one side you should install it with the textured side inwards: less dirt collects on the inside, which makes cleaning easier.

but the design is so uncomplicated that it will be easy for you to draw the pattern to whatever size you like.

Do be aware that a stained glass window is much heavier than an ordinary window.

METHOD

1 Make two full-sized drawings of your design (called cartoons). Draw all the outlines 2mm ($^1/_{16}$in) thick as this represents the core of the came. When you cut your glass, you should cut inside these lines.

2 Place your board, with its surround at the bottom and left-hand side, on a firm surface.

3 Pull a length of came – most easily done in a vice. Do not pull more than you are about to use, because it cannot be pulled a second time.

4 Cut a length of came to go along the bottom of the frame (the easiest way to cut came is with a slight rocking motion). Cut another length of came for along the left-hand side. At corners came can be either mitred or abutted together, whichever you prefer.

5 Position your cartoon on the board and stick it down with a glue stick to hold it in place.

6 Cut your first piece of glass: it must be the piece for the left-hand bottom corner. Place it in position on the frame, pushing it firmly into the came.

7 Keep first piece of glass firmly in position by hammering in a couple of horseshoe nails around the edges.

8 Measure the length of came required to go round it and cut came to that length. Remove the nails, place the came around the glass, and re-secure it in position with nails. Do not put nails directly against the came as it will damage it: use small offcuts of came between the nail and the came around the glass as protection.

9 Build up your pattern in this way. You must work from the bottom left-hand corner and finish at the top right-hand corner. This will allow you to alter your design slightly when you come to insert the final pieces, should you find – through slight errors in cutting – that your panel is either too large or too small.

10 After you have inserted four or five pieces of glass, check that they are firmly inside the came and tap them home using a wedge-shaped piece of wood.

HELPFUL HINT

Glass-cutting: if the glass is clear enough, place your design under the glass and cut inside the black outlines. If your glass is dark or opaque, or if you prefer this method, cut all the shapes out of thin card and use them as templates on top of the glass. Remember always to leave 2mm ($^1/_{16}$in) for the core of the came.

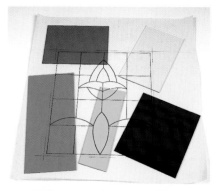

The plates of glass laid over the cartoon, or template

Scoring the glass with a single-wheel glass cutter

Snapping the glass along the scored line

Using the grozing pliers to cut curves

The first piece in place

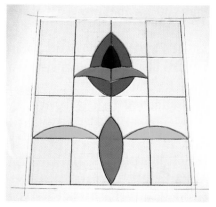

Assembling the panel to make sure that everything fits

11 Finally add the cames at the top and right-hand side. Hold them firmly in place with nails and then tap them firmly into place as described above.

SOLDERING

12 Clean all the joints to be soldered with either a fine wire brush or wire wool. Apply a small amount of liquid flux with a brush, or use a tallow candle.

13 Hold your stick of solder just above the join. Apply the hot soldering iron so that a blob of solder falls onto the flux. If you have not cleaned the came sufficiently the solder will not stay on the join. Moreover, if you forget to flux the solder will fall off the came. If there is insufficient flux the solder will not run enough to make a good join, and if there is too much the result will be an untidy and unnecessarily large join.

14 After you have soldered one side turn the panel over and solder the other side. Remember to clean your soldering iron on a wet piece of cloth while you are working. You must not just pick up the panel: instead you should slide it to the edge of the board and then gently turn it over.

CEMENTING

Having experimented with various ways of cementing or puttying stained-glass panels, I believe this is the easiest. If you are using your panel as a hanging ornament, it is not necessary to cement it.

15 Add a small amount of black watercolour or poster paint to the ready-mixed filler to darken it and then push it between the glass and the came using either a brush or an old palette knife. Take care, if you are using a palette knife, not to scratch the glass.

16 Then use lead cement. This is slightly messier than the Tetrion, and if it is very oily you will need to brush on some whiting powder to absorb excess oil.

17 Turn over the panel and cement the other side.

18 Clean away any excess filler/putty with a Nova tool, taking great care to clear the corners. Brush away all debris with a scrubbing brush and burnish the lead with newspaper. Your panel is now waterproof.

Supporting the design with horseshoe nails

Cutting the came to size...

...and pushing it into place with an oyster knife

Soldering the lead came

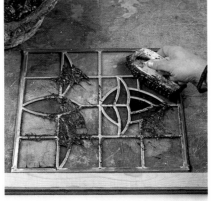

Applying cement to the finished panel

Drying the cement with whiting powder

Picking out excess cement from the edges of the came

Brushing the surface clean

19 Blacken all the leads by applying black patina or zebrite with a brush. Continue to brush until the leads begin to glow: the darkened lead will greatly enhance the colours of the glass.

If your panel is very large it will have to be supported.
1 You will have to insert a reinforcing bar into the wooden framework of your window. Mark on your panel where this will come.

2 Solder copper wires to the came of your panel where the bar will cross at 15cm (6in) intervals.

3 If you have removed your original window, insert your reinforcing bar (or bars if your window is really large) at approx. 50cm [20in] intervals across your window space, and put your panel in place from the outside. Twist the holding wires round the bar. If you are not removing your original window but using your panel as double glazing, you will have to put in your reinforcing bar after positioning your panel.

Once your panel is complete, clean it as you would a traditional window. Attach hanging hooks (see page 109) and finally attach a chain for hanging. If your panel is very heavy you must use H came for the outside border and use a continuous wire round the whole panel inside the outside rim of the came. Solder it into position at approx. 10cm (4in) intervals.

Rearing Horse panel

A modernistic design for a panel featuring a rearing horse – it measures 45 x 65cm (18 x 26in). A panel of this size will need no extra support before it is inserted into a window space or used as a secondary glazing panel inside an existing window: anything bigger would. It could also be framed with wood to make a fire screen.

METHOD
Follow steps **1–18** of the method for a traditional stained-glass window on pages 58–61.

MATERIALS

Coloured glass

Several lengths of lead came. (Estimate the amount you will need by measuring along your black lines with a piece of string. Although it is available in various widths, if your cutting is not too accurate it is best to use 5mm (³⁄₁₆in)

approx. 3 sticks solder

Chipboard (5cm [2in] larger than finished panel) with raised wooden surround at base and up left-hand side

approx. 12 horseshoe nails (ordinary nails will do but they are not so easy to remove from your board as horseshoe nails)

Ready-mixed Tetrion all-purpose filler

Lead-light cement

Modern designs are bold and unfussy

Fire Screen – Lady with an Umbrella

I made a fire screen using a stained-glass panel. First of all I made a wooden frame using picture-framing. Having inserted the stained-glass panel, I nailed on a 2cm (³⁄₄in) batten at the back to hold it in position.

I bought four ornate black iron brackets (intended for use with hanging flower baskets) and secured them at the bottom of the frame: i.e. two pairs of brackets fixed back-to-back to form sturdy 'feet'.

The Madonna and Child panel
(above) is mainly comprised of
straight edges and is relatively
simple to make.

The Peacock (right) is more
elaborate, and you would need many
hours to complete it.

Hanging panels

Here are two further designs that you might like to enlarge and use as cartoons for stained-glass panels – with the details painted onto the glass as they have been for centuries but in modern non-firing paint. (For the traditional method, see page 79.) It is possible to paint very intricate designs using these paints – mistakes can be removed with thinner. They should not be used for external windows, however.

The Nativity scene is incredibly easy because it is made up entirely of straight lines. The idea for Lady with a Hat panel came from Rodin's sculpture in the Rodin Museum, Paris.

METHOD

1 Enlarge your chosen design to the size of your finished piece and make a copy for reference. Construct your leaded panel using the method described for the Victorian-style window panel. When constructing the Lady with a Hat panel I made the flowers for her hat using the copper-foil method and

Nativity scene, using straight lines only

Lady with a Hat - based on Rodin's sculpture in the Rodin Museum, Paris

then used the assembled posy as one piece of glass and inserted it in the panel with lead came.

2 Draw all the details in black on one of your full-sized cartoons.

3 Using an easel or light box (see below), or just laying your panel on a light-coloured surface, place this cartoon under your leaded panel.

4 Make sure that your workplace is well ventilated. Then, with a small brush (no.1 or 2), lightly paint all the details onto the glass. I used only Deka Black and White on the Nativity panel. On the Lady with a Hat I have used red transparent paint for the lips and blue for the eyes as well as black for the outlines.

Light up your panel

MATERIALS

Traditional lead-camed stained-glass panel – no need to cement the panel

Light Box (for instructions, see page 12) – if light is to be left on for long periods, it is advisable to increase the depth of the box (up to 10cm [4in]) as this will prevent overheating

Dimmer switch (optional)

One delightful way to show off a stained-glass panel is to fix it to a light box. It is also a very useful device where no natural light is available. You can fix the light box to a wall in a dark corner and it will soon become an attractive focal point, especially at night.

METHOD

Make up as for light table (see page 12), although you may like to substitute small candle-type light bulbs. Four bulbs will be required to give an even all-over light.

Light treatment: this parrot glows vividly when its colours are enhanced either by natural or strong artificial light.

Design your own rose window

Round windows in the twelfth century were roughly hewn in stone. In the thirteenth century the designs became more intricate. The patterns chiefly depicted flower petals, so the term rose window came into being. Many thirteenth-century Gothic cathedrals have beautiful rose windows: Wells, Lincoln, Salisbury and Winchester, to name but a few in England. Many of these lovely round windows still remain.

Modern buildings and especially houses do not generally have round windows. I have overcome this problem by positioning my circular rose window within a rectangular surround of plain glass. While I still have the illusion of a rose window, the whole can be fitted into a rectangular space. I have incorporated the well-known tulip design which is used a great deal for Tiffany lampshades.

MATERIALS

90 x 90cm (36 x 36in) coloured glass for main part of design

Small pieces of glass in complementary colours

Came, solder and flux

Chipboard with raised wooden surround up left-hand side and along bottom

METHOD

1 Enlarge the design to the size you require. Either photocopy it or, which is the easiest way, square up the design. Divide my design into small squares and then divide up a piece of paper the size of your window into the same number of squares. Copy the design, working through the individual elements of one square at a time. Make two drawings – one to use as your cutting template and one to put on your board.

2 Decide on your colour scheme and start cutting the glass. Place into position on the board and progress your pattern as for traditional came work (see pages 59-61).

3 Surround each piece of glass with came and hammer gently in place. Secure with horseshoe nails.

4 Complete as for traditional panel.

HELPFUL HINT

As this window is essentially to show a circular design it might be a good idea, in this instance, to cut all your coloured pieces first in order to ensure that your design is perfect when assembled. Any slight error in the completed circle can be adjusted within your rectangle with the plain pieces of glass.

Glass door panel

MATERIALS

1.8 x 1.8m (72 x 72in) white frosted glass 3mm (⅛in) thick

46 x 46cm (18 x 18in) dark blue glass 3mm (⅛in) thick

46 x 46cm (18 x 18in) red glass 3mm (⅛in) thick

46 x 46cm (18 x 18in) light amber (or yellow opalescent) glass 3mm (⅛in) thick

30 x 30cm (12 x 12in) pink glass 3mm (⅛in) thick

30 x 30cm (12 x 12in) light blue 3mm (⅛in) thick

30x 30cm (12 x 12in) light green 3mm (⅛in) thick

30 x 30cm (12 x 12in) dark green 3mm (⅛in) thick

2 metal rods 56cm (22in) long and 6mm (¼in) in diameter

61cm (24in) copper wire for ties

approx. 9 lengths of 6mm (¼in) H lead came

Solder

Zebrite

HELPFUL HINT

The most suitable glass for an exterior door is glass which is textured on one side. Instal the glass so that the textured side is on the inside – it allows for easier cleaning.

Once you become really at ease with stained glass as a medium and all your available window space has been enhanced with it, the next project to tackle must be a door. Many houses have doors with frosted glass panels that let in the light. Sometimes the glass is divided by wooden bars into two or three sections. With this type of door it is very easy to remove the old glass and wooden crossbars and replace them with an original stained glass panel.

When I removed the old glass from my door I was left with a hole 120 x 56cm (47 x 22in). There was a solid wood panel at the bottom of the door and a wooden frame 95mm (3¾in) wide around the hole. Because it was a back door in constant use, I needed this extra wooden framework to support the stained glass panel – when finished, it would be very heavy.

METHOD

1 Measure the size of the panel accurately: it is better to have the panel slightly loose-fitting than a tight fit.

2 Unless you have lots of space and many willing hands to help you turn your panel over it is better to make the panel in two separate sections. I made my door in three sections. This gave me the opportunity to strengthen my finished panel in one of two ways: either by joining the sections together with a 12mm (½in) lead came, which has a steel rod running through its core, or by inserting two metal bars into the wooden surround behind the panel and securing them with ties. I decided to use this latter method.

3 Make full-size cartoons of the three sections.

4 Start with bottom section and follow instructions as for traditional stained-glass window (see pages 59-60). Do not place any lead at the top of the section, and cut the lead which reaches up to the top of section 2mm (³⁄₃₂in) shorter than the glass.

5 Make the second section in the same way as the first section and then make the third and final section with lead going all around it. Before completing the last section measure the total length of your three panels to check for size and make any necessary adjustments on this last section.

6 After cementing each section on both sides, attach tinned copper ties across where metal bars will go. Solder these wire ties to the lead came at approx. 10cm (4in) intervals.

7 Apply Zebrite to the lead with a soft cloth and polish.

HELPFUL HINT

If it is at all possible to remove the door completely you will find it much easier to insert the panel while the door is lying flat. Remember, though, that the completed door will be heavy and require two people to replace it.

Floral designs are a popular choice for door and window panels.

TO INSERT THE PANEL INTO THE DOOR

8 Remove the old glass from the door and clean the surround. As you will not be able to make a large panel very quickly it is advisable to leave your old glass in place until your panel is complete.

9 If the door is an external one, nail new wooden beading to the outside-facing part of the door. If it is an internal room door, put the beading to the side facing inwards.

10 Place the bottom section into the opening pressing it firmly against the new beading. Check that the panel does not fit too tightly; if tight, file off some of the lead came.

11 Put second section in position ensuring that the bottom 12mm (½in) H came fits snugly over all the glass at the top of the bottom section. Then put the top section into position. Solder all joins where the sections meet.

12 Cut two lengths of metal bar to fit across the opening. Place metal bar over lead holding soldered-on ties. Twist the ties around the metal bar and cut off any untidy ends.

13 Cut the top and the bottom beadings for the door and hammer them into position. Then cut the two side beadings, leaving spaces for the metal rods, and hammer side beadings into door.

14 Give stained-glass panel a final polish and re-hang the door.

Pair of modern abstract door panels

The twentieth century produced a revival in the popularity of stained glass. After World War II stained-glass artists were much in demand to replace windows damaged in churches and cathedrals. This renovation completed, the artists are now enhancing modern buildings with stained glass that comple§ments modern architecture. The straight lines of new buildings demand either bold designs or straight lines in stained-glass work.

More and more domestic premises are once again being decorated with stained-glass windows. It is often either necessary or attractive to continue a design from one window to the next. For instance, I have included here a design for the glazing of a large double door. The wooden frame between the two windows, each measuring 51 x 38cm (20 x 15in), is 17.5cm (7in) wide so the design has to be bold enough to pass over this without losing its sense of continuity. Various colour schemes were tried on my original drawings before a final decision was made. The large circles are red and give a good focal point to the eye: they are carried through from one panel to the next.

Although there are lots of curves they are large and therefore quite easy to cut. It is also much easier, when cutting circles, if you have a circular glass cutter.

Richly coloured swirls in a domestic setting

Table lantern

MATERIALS

Coloured glass pieces (as many colours as
are compatible with each other)

H came

C came

90° corner came (usually sold in 2m
(6 1/2ft) lengths; 7x3mm (1/4x1/8in) or
13x4.5mm (1/2x3/16in)

approx. 30 x 30cm (12 x 12in) board with
raised wooden border up left-hand side
and along bottom edge

Flux, solder, patina

H aving made traditional panels with came it is quite exciting to
make something three-dimensional using this technique. This
table lantern is quite complicated, so do not attempt it until you have
made several panels using came.

Decide first of all which type of glass best suits your needs.
Cathedral glass will be more vibrantly coloured but will show the
electrical fittings. Opalescent glass will hide the fittings, is slightly
lighter in weight and dulls down the light shining through the mixture
of colours. I have chosen antique glass, and have made two sides
predominantly red and amber and the other two sides mostly blue and
green. I have also made each side of my lantern different, while you
might prefer to have the same pattern on all four sides.

METHOD

1 Trace a design (or a series) from those shown – or design your own.
Make a copy of it. Place one cartoon (drawing) onto your board and use
the other as your glass cutting guide.

2 Cut glass: either place the glass over your design or cut the cartoon
into individual templates. Remember to cut inside the black lines, as
these represent the core of the came.

 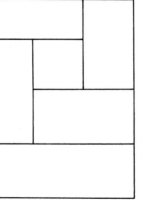 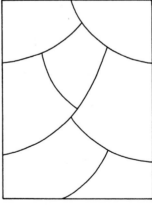 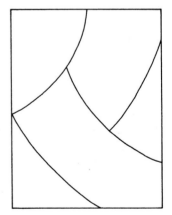

Some suggestions for table lantern designs

TOP OF TABLE LANTERN

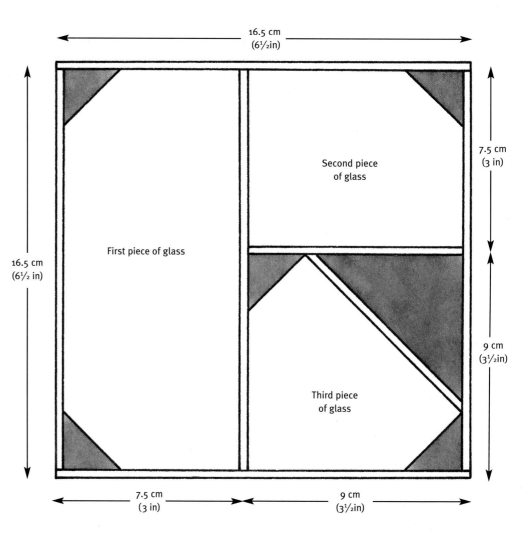

3 Place C came along the bottom of the board and corner came up the left-hand side of board. Where it abuts at the bottom corner the corner came goes above the C came (the corner came is placed with the open 'heart' upwards): this is because you want the C came to make a continuous band along the bottom of the finished lantern.

4 Construct your panel as per the instructions for a traditional lead-came panel (pages 59-61), starting at the bottom left-hand side and finishing with the piece of glass at the top right-hand corner.

5 Measure your completed panel and adjust size at this stage.

6 Put corner came along top – open 'heart' to top. Leave the right-hand side without any came. The edges of the glass should protrude approx. 3mm (⅛in) outside all the came pieces in order to allow it to fit into the corner came of adjoining side. Solder all joins.

7 Make three more panels in the same way.

TO ASSEMBLE THE LAMP

8 Stand two sides together and push protruding glass into the corner came. An extra pair of hands and patience are both useful at this stage. It is also useful to spot solder at the top join while these pieces are still standing up.

9 Check that your angles are 90°: lay one side flat on your bench and support the upright side with books or something similar – the spot solder keeps your work in the correct position while you lay it down. Then solder at the joins.

10 Put third side in place and proceed as for second side. Keep checking that your angles are correct.

11 Putting the fourth side into position requires patience again. Once you are satisfied with the construction, spot solder at the top while the lantern is still in a standing position. Solder joins inside and out. You now have an open-ended box that should support itself even though it is lying on its side.

12 Stand the lantern upright again and measure your top. Cut your glass as shown in the diagram. You might like to try other designs for the top: experiment with pieces of cardboard. You will notice that I have left holes at the top. I feel this is advisable because even a low-wattage bulb gives off a certain amount of heat.

13 It is most important that you follow the sequence for placing the glass pieces for the top in the correct order, or you will find that the last piece will not fit. You must remember all the time that glass is not flexible. Place the first piece into position on the lantern, push hard into corner came, and, if you have difficulty inserting the glass, open the 'heart'. Cut H came, place it along this piece of glass and solder each end to the top of the lantern. Repeat for the second piece.

14 Cut last piece of glass and insert it into the corner came.

TO INSERT A LIGHT BULB AND COMPLETE THE LANTERN

15 Connect a plugged flex to a ceiling-fitting bayonet bulb holder and attach that to a wooden rose (used for ceiling fittings).

16 Screw rose to a 25 x 25 x 5cm (10 x 10 x 2in) block of wood to add weight, and place under lantern. Trail the wire through the space left at the bottom of the lantern.

Advanced projects

Once you have mastered the basic stained glass processes you may wish to tackle some more ambitious work, whether it is painting on glass in the traditional manner, combining the techniques you have already used or incorporating your panels in, for example, pieces of furniture. This section also encourages you to create your own designs for panels, terrariums and other projects.

PAINTING ON GLASS

With our hanging panels (page 65) we painted on glass, but we used modern non-firing paints, a practice which purists would no doubt regard as cheating. The traditional method of painting on glass is altogether more complicated, involving three separate processes, and for that reason it isn't often included in books for beginners. I hope nonetheless that the following example will inspire you to investigate more closely.

Tools

1 *magnifying glass for sketching*

2 *large badger brush*

3 *small blender brush*

4 *small badger brush*

5 *two hog brushes*

6 *tracing or rigour brush*

7 *knitting needle for highlighting lines*

8 *tile for mixing pigment*

9 *water container and dropper*

10 *handrest (see photograph, page 81)*

11 *pallette knife*

12 *pencil for sketching*

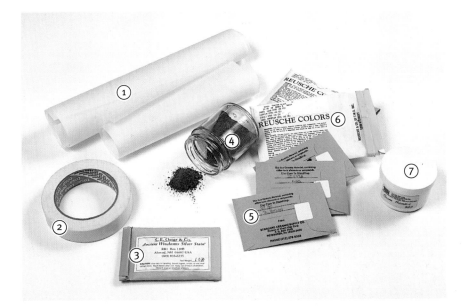

Materials

1 *tracing paper*

2 *masking tape*

3 *silver stain*

4 *tracing colours*

5 *transparent colours*

6 *packets of pigment*

7 *gum arabic*

Painting the Bridge of Sighs

MINIMUM REQUIREMENTS

Kiln for firing

FOR TRACING

Long-haired sable brush

Tracing pigment – either black or brown

Palette knife

Tile on which to mix pigments

FOR SHADING

Shading pigment

Badger brush

FOR STIPPLING

Small sponge or dry brush

Knitting needle, or something similar

FOR STAINING

(stains are much more expensive than shading and tracing pigments)

Oxide of silver (silver nitrate) stain

Brush (badger brush is suitable)

Note Transparent glass colour is a vitreous paint sold in powder form and applied to the back of the glass. I do not propose to deal with colour painting, as a great deal of time and experimenting is required to perfect this technique.

A ll the panels that have been described so far have relied largely on the lead or copper-foiled lines to define the design. Painting on glass is very different. It requires specialized knowledge, and a comprehensive description would fill many pages. The three stages are tracing; shading and matting; and the application of colour. The glass is fired after each stage.

You can, of course, create your own design, drawing your cartoon freehand, but many of us will choose to make a copy of something 'found'. For our example, I have chosen the Bridge of Sighs at St John's College, Cambridge. Once you have fired your tracing of the scene you will be covering everything with a thin layer of paint (shading) and then picking out the highlights (stippling) with a sponge and a sharp point. After the next firing you will turn the glass over and apply stain to the reverse side to produce your finished panel.

TRACING

In glass painting you should ideally use an easel and support your work against a sheet of plate glass, although it is possible to work on a table providing that the surface is fairly light. You trace the main outlines of your design on to your glass from your cartoon, which is placed underneath the glass. Use a long-haired sable brush, and practise on a spare piece of glass before you attempt to trace your chosen design. The pigment used for your tracing is usually black or brown. Only a thin application is necessary because the tracing is opaque.

MIXING PIGMENT

Put a small amount of pigment on your tile. Flick just sufficient gum arabic (I find the powdered sort the easiest to use) from the end of a palette knife to lightly cover your paint. The gum arabic is necessary to stick the paint to the glass while firing. Add water and mix the paint until you have a smooth, runny paste.

FIRING

Place your work flat on your kiln shelf. The initial firing is at 660°C (1220°F).

SHADING

When you have fired your tracing outlines you will need to add shading pigments to add tone and highlights to your painting. Mix your shading pigment with gum arabic as for the tracing paints: use brown and grey-green. With your badger brush, brush a light layer of paint over the whole of your design using both horizontal and vertical strokes. When the paint is dry to touch, rub the palm of your hand over it lightly to give it a translucent appearance, which will look particularly good when it has been fired.

Make a cartoon of the design - in this case the Bridge of Sighs at St John's College, Cambridge University.

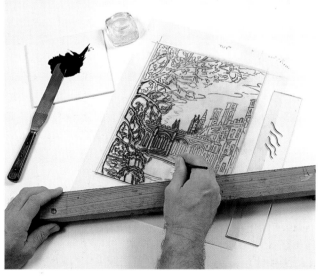

Lay your glass over the cartoon, and trace the design with a long-haired sable brush. This is followed by the first firing.

After firing, shade the picture by brushing a light layer of paint all over it.

When the paint is almost dry, create highlights with a dry brush or sponge. Note the knitting needle for creating fine lines.

You can make the effect even more emphatic by stippling the pigment when it is almost dry – and before firing – with a dry brush or sponge. If you want to create highlights, use a dental stick or, for an even finer line, the point of a thin plastic knitting needle. Fire at 640°C (1184°F). You can, if you wish, leave your painted glass as finished at this stage.

Note: Firing temperatures may vary with different paints and in different kilns, so the temperatures given here are guidelines only. You will have to experiment for optimum results.

STAINING AND COLOURING

Before you attempt staining on a particular object you intend to keep, it is best to practise on a spare piece of glass.

Mix a small amount of stain with water until you have a fairly runny consistency. With a blender brush (or wide brush with short soft hairs, brush onto the back of your glass – not on the surface which you have used for tracing and shading. Brush horizontally or vertically so that no brushstrokes are visible. Let the stain flow over the glass. You will find, after the next and final firing, that the colour will appear much deeper

Place the glass in the kiln for its second firing.

Turn the glass over and stain your picture, using a brush or sponge. Fire it once more.

where you have applied thicker layers of stain and very delicate where only a thin layer has been applied. Use oxide of silver to produce exciting colours from champagne to rich amber. Fire once more at 550°C (1022°F).

New and more user-friendly products and materials are constantly being brought on to the market. It is possible today to purchase painting pigments, for example, which only require water for mixing and which are extremely easy to use. There is also stain on the market which can be fired at the same temperature as the tracing and shading pigments, and this allows the whole process to be completed in one firing. I would suggest, however, that you practise using the two/three firing method until you are used to both the pigments and your kiln.

ETCHING

In this process hydrofluoric acid is used to remove a thin layer of flashed glass to reveal the colour of the glass underneath. I have not included an etching project in this book because of the safety risks: poisonous fumes are an unavoidable part of the process and the acid will burn unless handled with extreme care.

THE FUSED-GLASS TECHNIQUE

Fused glass is glass which has been heated sufficiently to melt into another piece lying under it or partly touching it. When fusing glass it is necessary to use glass of the same type (compatible), or the different types will expand and contract at different rates during the heating and cooling process, and the glass will crack.

Glass fuses at a temperature of 760°–845°C (1400°F–1550°F) depending on the type. A kiln is essential, which means for practical reasons that fused glass is not for the beginner: it is a complex process, too, and cannot be dealt with completely in a few paragraphs.

If you are in a position to try to work with fused glass, you must experiment with different types of glass and get to know your own kiln, because most kilns have cold spots. Keep a record of all your tests.

Fused mobiles

MATERIALS

Small pieces of light- and dark-coloured glass

Nichrome wire (wire with a very high melting point) to make hanging hooks – obtainable from pottery suppliers

Access to kiln

Try making a small mobile to start with. It is great fun. To begin with it is best to use special fusing glass and follow the manufacturer's advice as to optimum temperature.

METHOD

1 Prepare the kiln by brushing shelf primer evenly over each shelf. Use first horizontal and then vertical brushstrokes until you have a layer of primer approximately 3mm (⅛in) thick. This is to prevent the glass from sticking to the shelves.

2 Draw design. Cut glass.

3 Place glass pieces on to bat. This requires patience, as each piece of glass must be on top of another piece, partially touching it.

4 Place small pieces of bent nichrome wire at top of the mobile and 'hold down' with a small triangle of glass. This small piece will melt into the glass underneath and secure the nichrome wire hook.

5 Put the shelf into the kiln with a very steady hand – otherwise your glass pieces will slide off each other and will not fuse.

6 Bring kiln up to required temperature.

There is another way to make a fused glass mobile. Cut a base piece of light-coloured glass and place darker-coloured pieces on top into your desired pattern, and fire. This method is much easier, as there is no need for small pieces of glass to be touching. The whole picture will fuse into the base.

Cupboard with stained glass doors

MATERIALS

Approx. 120 x 120cm (48 x 48in) in total coloured glass 3mm (⅛in) thick (depending on colour choice)

Roll of copper foil 5mm (⁷⁄₃₂in) wide to make wide-seam soldered joins (which I antiqued with copper patina)

Stick solder (approx 5 sticks should be sufficient)

FOR THE CUPBOARD

Approx. 23 x 200cm (9 x 80in) veneered blockboard

58 x 43cm (23 x 17in) translucent plastic for back panel

280cm (112in) angle moulding 2.5cm (1in) wide into which you will insert your glass panels

280cm (112in) wood 12.5 x 20mm (½ x ¾in) to place behind panels to hold them in place in the mouldings

4 hinges

2 door catches

4 rubber feet

Glue, nails and screws

Piece of wood for centre front

METHOD: COPPER-FOIL

Once you have mastered the copper-foil technique it is interesting to discover how many things you can make with this method. I decided to make a cupboard with stained-glass doors. As my design has lots of small curved pieces, using came would have been impractical and, anyway, the weight of the came would have been too heavy for the small hinges on the doors.

METHOD

1 Draw two identical full-sized (25.5 x 40cm/10 x 16in) cartoons of the chosen design. The drawing lines should be 1mm (1/32in) thick to represent the space which will be taken up by the copper foil. Remember to number each piece.

2 Cut one design into individual pieces, cutting inside the drawing line. Leave the other design complete, as you will need this to place your work on as you progress. It is rather like fixing together a jigsaw, and because of this it is helpful if you colour your complete design before you start.

3 Either put your pattern piece (template) under the glass if you are using cathedral glass or, if you are using opalescent glass, stick it on top of the glass with gluestick. Cut your glass (see page 14).

4 Place each cut piece of glass onto your complete design. If you have to remove the pieces of glass at any time, remember to number them – use a permanent ink pen.

5 After you have cut all your glass, foil and tin each piece.

6 Place foiled and tinned pieces on to your complete design.

7 Make a wooden frame to hold your work while you are soldering. The board (chipboard is suitable) should be 5cm (2in) larger than your cartoon all round and should have a raised border along the left-hand side and along the bottom. This will steady your work and ensure that the angles and sides are correct.

8 Stick all your pieces into position with masking tape. Put the tape across the centre of adjoining edges, leaving the corners free.

9 Spot solder at the corners of adjoining edges.

HELPFUL HINT

If you want to use the panels as decorative panels to hang in a window, you will need to surround each with C came and attach hooks and chain (see instructions on page 109).

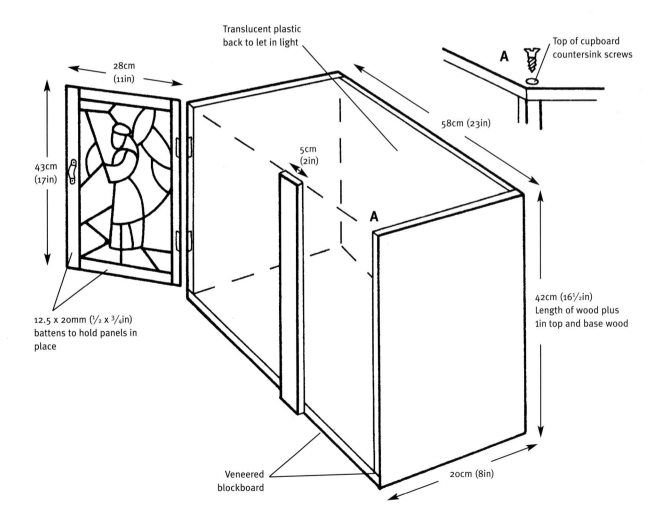

28cm (11in)

43cm (17in)

Translucent plastic back to let in light

5cm (2in)

A

58cm (23in)

Top of cupboard countersink screws

42cm (16½in)
Length of wood plus 1in top and base wood

20cm (8in)

12.5 x 20mm (½ x ¾in) battens to hold panels in place

Veneered blockboard

10 When you have satisfied yourself that the design is correct and that all the angles at the corners of the panel are right angles, seam solder each piece, removing the masking tape as you go.

11 Bead solder.

12 When you have soldered one side of your panel, turn it over and solder the other side.

13 Apply black or copper patina to the seams with a soft cloth.

14 Clean the whole panel by washing it in washing-up liquid and then rinsing it in clear water.

TO MAKE THE CUPBOARD

15 Make frames for your glass door panels with moulding. Mitre the corners and glue the pieces together. Insert your panel and secure it with the 12.5 x 20mm (½ x ¾in) wood strip. This should be cut to length to make an inside surround. Glue it to the inside of the moulding and reinforce with small nails at the corners. At this stage each door should measure 28 x 43cmm (11 x 17in).

16 Saw two 58.5cm (23in) lengths of blockboard 23cm (9in) wide and two 42cm (16½in). Glue and screw together.

17 Glue two pieces of wood (50 x 20mm [2 x ¾in]) to the centre front – one at the top and the other at the bottom .

18 Attach hinges to the doors and fix the doors to the cupboard.

19 Nail on the translucent back to let in the light so that it shines through the front, displaying all the bright colours. You can also fix a small fluorescent tube inside the cupboard, which will make the colours shine even more brightly on to the surrounding surfaces.

20 Fix door catches to doors and centre wooden strip.

21 Screw four rubber feet to the base. The glass doors are quite heavy, so the front two feet must be placed well forward or the cupboard might tilt forward.

22 Sandpaper finish and wax polish.

CHOOSING YOUR COLOURS

The beauty of stained glass lies in the fact that the daylight shining through the coloured glass makes the picture and its surroundings vibrate with colour. This colour changes in mood as the morning light turns to bright sunlight and then back again to dim dusk. In choosing the theme and the colours to be used in a stained glass window two facts have to be considered:

a. Does the theme of the window fit in with its surroundings?

b. Where does the sun rise and set in relation to the site of the window?

- Windows facing east get the morning sun and those facing west the setting sun, so that reds, oranges and yellows will be further 'warmed' by the sunlight. Windows facing north and south get more even light during the day, so the warm colours are not necessary if a glowing light is expected from your stained glass window.

- The colder colours of blue and green will be brought more to life if the most sunshine possible is allowed to flow through them.

- However, seasons change and many more days are without sunshine: this, too, should be taken into consideration when choosing your colours.

- The rule applied to painting that warm colours bring the subject forward and colder colours make things appear to recede does not apply rigidly to stained glass work. This is because the black came line breaks up the colours and also this allows colours which normally would not blend well together to be used in the same window.

- A window made entirely with warm colours or a window made using only cool colours will give a pleasing effect. On a small scale I have used this principle with both my table lantern (page 72) and the appliqué candle holder, (page.50).

OPALESCENT VERSUS TRANSPARENT

At one time no stained glass window had any opalescent glass in it. Now, however, a combination of both is used quite satisfactorily. If opalescent glass is used to surround transparent glass, this will make the transparent glass appear brighter.

- Opalescent glass is useful if complete privacy is required for a window.

- If the brilliance of medieval glass is required, only transparent glass should be used.

PROJECTS USING COMBINED TECHNIQUES

I f you now feel at home with lead came work, copper foil, appliqué and painting on glass, why not consider bringing all your skills together? Here are some ideas to start you off – afterwards your own ingenuity should keep you busy with a host of imaginative projects!

Panel – Flowers in a Window

MATERIALS

Copy of design

20 x 20cm (8 x 8in) clear glass 3mm (⅛in) thick

Small pieces of coloured glass (cullet)

Approx. 60cm (24in) of C lead came

5cm (2in) copper-covered fuse wire for making hanging hooks

Solder and flux (to join C lead round glass)

Glass bond

Non-firing glass paints (I use Deka and Pebeo)

USING APPLIQUÉ AND NON-FIRING PAINT

You can have great fun and achieve good results by combining appliqué with painting on glass. A circle makes an excellent base for your project: I have drawn a vase of flowers standing on a window ledge, framing it with the curtains hanging down each side.

METHOD

1 Cut a circle 18cm (7in) diameter from your clear glass. The easiest way, of course, is with a circular cutter, but if you do not have access to one then the best way is to draw a circle on a piece of paper, stick this under your glass with a glue stick and then cut 10mm (⅜in) at a time around the circumference. The smaller your cuts, the neater your circle will be. Finish the circle using a grinder.

2 Put C came around the glass circle and solder together at the top. Add hanging hooks (see page 109).

3 With your design under your glass follow instructions for earlier appliqué objects (page 49), but in this case break your glass into really small pieces. The simplest way to do this is to place some small pieces of glass between several layers of newspaper and then to hit the newspaper hard with a hammer. The glass will shoot out, so it is

The design under its circle of glass with lead came surround

Small fragments of glass are stuck on the design to build up the picture

After painting, finish the project by grouting between the pieces of glass

extremely important to have enough newspaper padding before you start to hammer.

4 Stick fragments of glass on to your circle to form curtains, a window ledge, a vase, flowers, a bowl and fruit.

5 Paint the remainder of the window with non-firing paints.

6 Grout between the pieces of glass. Gently wash the whole panel, taking care not to wash the painted areas too vigorously.

Round mirror with appliqué clown

USING COPPER FOIL AND APPLIQUÉ
The easiest way to decorate a mirror with stained glass is to combine the appliqué and copper-foil methods. I am sure this clown mirror will delight child and adult alike.

MATERIALS

Round mirror 25cm (10in) in diameter with two holes drilled in it

2 copies of the clown design, one drawn on thin card

Small length of tinned copper wire

Small pieces of red, blue and black opalescent glass

5mm ($7/_{32}$in) copper foil

2 rawl plugs and 2 screws

Epoxy resin

METHOD

1 Cut out your clown design in thin cardboard, cutting inside the drawn lines.

2 Lay the template on your glass, and either cut directly around it or draw round it with a fine liner pen and cut freehand round these areas.

3 Foil land tin all the pieces, put and the clown on a flat surface and solder all the pieces together.

4 Mix epoxy resin following the manufacturer's instructions.

5 Put mixed resin on the back of the clown, carefully position it on your mirror and hold it down firmly for a few seconds.

6 Make up a selection of balloons in any sequence you fancy and stick them on to the mirror.

7 Cut pieces of tinned copper wire and, using solder, attach one end to a balloon and the other to the clown's arm leaving a short length hanging down.

8 Add patina, leaving it silver-coloured. Wash in washing-up solution to remove surplus flux and patina.

Tiffany-style lampshade

USING COPPER-FOIL AND LEAD

As we saw on page 40, it is possible to make a Tiffany-style lampshade without the use of a mould. Use a wooden triangle as described for that project.

METHOD

1 Trace the design onto thin cardboard with a felt-tipped pen.

2 Cut out each piece of the pattern inside the drawing line: this makes allowance for your copper-foiled edges. These cardboard pieces are your templates.

3 This lampshade is made up of four pairs of panels. Place your template on the glass, draw around it and cut four identical pieces. Then turn the template over, draw around it and cut out four more identical pieces of glass.

4 Copper-foil and tin each piece.

5 Construct one panel. Arrange your tinned pieces on your wooden triangle according to the design. Spot, seam and bead solder.

6 Make up the rest of the panels, remembering to reverse four panels. (I have left a few pieces of glass out of my shade at the top for added ventilation and also to create a more unusual design.) Seam solder the second side of all the panels.

7 Lay the eight completed panels in a circle on a flat surface, remembering to turn over alternate panels to form the four pairs.

MATERIALS

91 x 91cm (36 x 36in) opalescent glass 3mm ($\frac{1}{8}$ in) thick (I used 30 x 30cm [12 x 12in] of red, green and grey)

5mm ($\frac{7}{32}$in) copper foil (small amount)

1 length C came

1 length 5mm ($\frac{3}{16}$in) H came

Thin cardboard from which to make templates (cereal packets are good)

Vase cap and finial

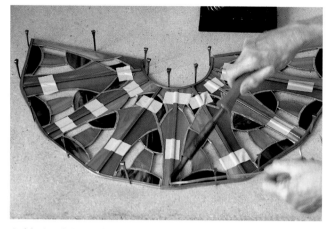

Soldering joints where C came touches H came. Note the masking tape to hold the lead in place.

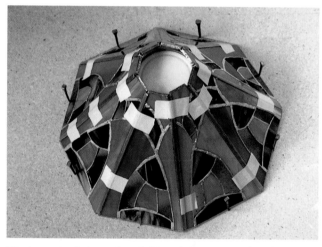

The lampshade turned upright and almost completed.

8 Cut a piece of H came to fit between two panels leaving 2mm (1/16in) of glass not covered at the top and bottom of shade. (See below.) Hold the lead in place with masking tape.

9 You need a tight-fitting C came to go around the bottom and top edges of the shade. Cut a length and push the glass firmly into the lead. Solder each joint where C lead touches H lead, scraping the surface of the lead before soldering.

10 Turn the shade over and solder the second side.

11 Curving it round until the edges meet, stand lampshade upright.

12 With someone to help you hold the shade at this stage, push the last piece of H came into place and solder.

13 The structure of your shade is complete. Now put black patina on the solder. Wash. Rub Zebrite into lead, and polish the whole shade with a soft cloth.

14 Attach the vase cap or, if you want to leave it open-topped, add a spider (see page 111).

Three techniques panel

Having mastered the three techniques of copper foil, appliqué and came, I thought a project using all three would be interesting. I have created a 30 x 30cm (12 x 12in) panel – to be used, looked at and looked through.

METHOD

1 Using the design on p. 96, draw two full-sized cartoons.

2 Cut all your pieces of glass for the base panel. Foil and tin them.

3 Place C came along the bottom and along the left-hand side of a board slightly larger than 30 x 30cm (12 x 12in) – against a surround, as for a traditional panel (see pages 58-62).

4 Assemble all pieces of the back panel, starting work at the bottom left-hand corner and spot soldering as you go until you reach the central 'cross'. Surround this with H came to give it more emphasis in the design, and then continue with the assembly.

5 Fit C came to to top and right-hand side of the panel.

MATERIALS

Oddments of glass

Copper foil

1 length of C came

1 length of H came

Glass bond

6 Solder each joint around the perimeter of the panel. Turn the panel over. Seam solder all copper-foil joins and spot solder all came joins.

7 Cut glass to form an open-topped box to fit on to the front of the panel:
  2 pieces 10 x 6.5cm (4 x 2½in) coloured glass for the front and base;
  2 pieces 6.5 x 6.5cm (2½ x 2½in) coloured glass for the sides;
  1 piece 10 x 6.5cm (4 x 2½in) plain glass for the back.

8 Foil and tin all the pieces, assemble as for the mirror-backed terrarium (page 20) and solder to the base panel in the position shown in the diagram below.

9 Cut glass for the shelf:
  2 pieces 4 x 4cm (2½ x 2½in) coloured glass with curved tops for the side of the shelf
  1 piece 10 x 4cm (4 x 2½in) plain glass for the back
  1 piece 9.5 x 4cm (3¾ x 2½in) coloured glass for the bottom
  1 piece 9.5 x 1.5cm (3¾ x ⅝in) coloured glass for the front

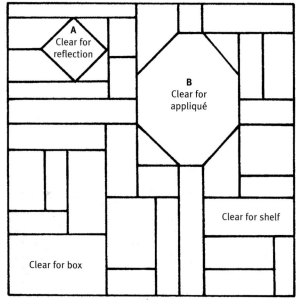

Complete base panel 30 x 30cm (12in x 12in)

10 Assemble the pieces and attach to the panel as for the box above.

11 In the plain panels marked A and B use small pieces of glass and glass bond to create your own appliqué designs. I have made a three-dimensional design in A and a flat design in B.

12 Wash the panel in a washing-up solution and rinse.

13 The panel is complete, because the box in the bottom left-hand corner is large enough to support the upright panel and you will not need to add a hanging chain. If you do add hanging hooks, use strong ones because the finished panel is quite heavy. Add flowers to the box and place small ornaments on the shelf to complete the display.

DESIGNING YOUR OWN PROJECTS

F ollowing other people's guidelines is the way that most of us begin, but once we have mastered the basic techniques it is satisfying to set off on our own voyages of discovery. Whatever your artistic flair, however, you need to recognise the especial requirements of designing for stained glass projects, and in this section I offer some basic hints to get you started.

Designing a terrarium

A fter you have made a few terrariums with bought patterns try designing your own.

METHOD FOR DESIGNING A MIRROR-BACKED TERRARIUM (see project, page 20)

1 Decide roughly what height and width you want the finished terrarium to be.

2 Decide on what type of base you want: square, rectangular, octagonal etc. I chose to use a rectangular base. Cut the shape of the base out of cardboard. If you think it looks too large or too small, simply alter the size.

3 You can make a full-sized cardboard mock-up, or maquette, but there is a simple way of making one which is much smaller than the finished terrarium but for which all the measurements will be easy to calculate. What you do is measure the base in inches and substitute centimetres. Thus, here the finished base measures 6 x 5in, so I cut mine 6 x 5cm.

4 Decide on the depth of the sides. Remember that you must have sides all round the base to hold in the earth. In this case the finished depth of the sides would be 5 x 7in so I cut my cardboard pattern 7 x 5cm. The finished front piece, to hold in earth, would measure 6 x 2½in, so I cut my pattern 6 x 2.5cm. Remember that if the sides of your terrarium are to be fixed on top of the base you must make the sides 3mm (⅛in) narrower to allow for the width of the glass.

5 Proceed like this, converting all your inches into centimetres. Design the roof next. Attach it to your model mock-up with adhesive tape. You now have a miniature model of your finished terrarium.

Using this very simple method you will be able to design any style of three-dimensional object.

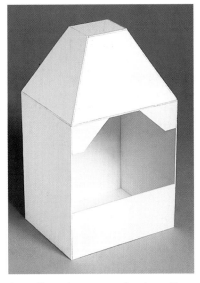

A cardboard maquette for the self-designed terrarium.

Designing a large oblong terrarium using lead came

MATERIALS

Base 22 x 13.5cm (8⅝ x 5⅜in)

End side panels (4) 22 x 13.5cm
(8⅝ x 5⅜in)

Centre front (1) 22 x 22cm (8⅝ x 8⅝in)
with sliding door (see diagram)

Centre back (1) 22 x 22cm (8⅝ x 8⅝in)

End roof panels (4) 17 x 16 x 13.5cm
(6⅝ x 6¼ x 5⅜in)

Centre roof panels (2) 22 x 17 x 16cm
(8⅝ x 6⅝ x 6¼in)

E ven when you have made lots of small terrariums, and either given them to your friends and relations for presents and/or sold them by the dozen at craft fairs, making a really large terrarium will still be a challenge. I have made one which is totally enclosed, with a sliding door at the centre of one side.

METHOD

1 Enlarge design to the required size. (I have suggested dimensions.)

2 Place the design under your glass and cut out all the pieces.

3 Cut the lead corner came to fit around the base pieces. Mitre your came at the corners.

4 Scrape the surface of the came before applying the flux and then solder all the joins, taking care that no solder flows inside the came.

5 Stand the sides in position in the lead groove, leaving out the front central upper piece.

6 Cut H came to fit all glass uprights leaving 3mm (⅛in) of glass uncovered at the top.

7 Place these pieces in position and solder to base (corner came). Attach C came to the top of the front bottom central panel.

8 Measure the size of your sliding door. Cut brass-coated C came to fit and solder this to both the front of the lead C came in central front panel and on to the sides of the H came. This brass-coated came will hold the sliding door.

9 Attach lead C came to the bottom of the top central piece of glass and solder in place.

10 Solder H came right around the top of the terrarium (below roof) both inside and outside.

HELPFUL HINT

Terrariums made with lead are more difficult to make waterproof than copper-foiled ones. It is advisable at this stage in your assembly, however, to cement your glass into the lead at the base and for 2.5cm (1in) up the sides (use either lead-light cement or tetrion). As an added precaution you can add transparent bath sealant.

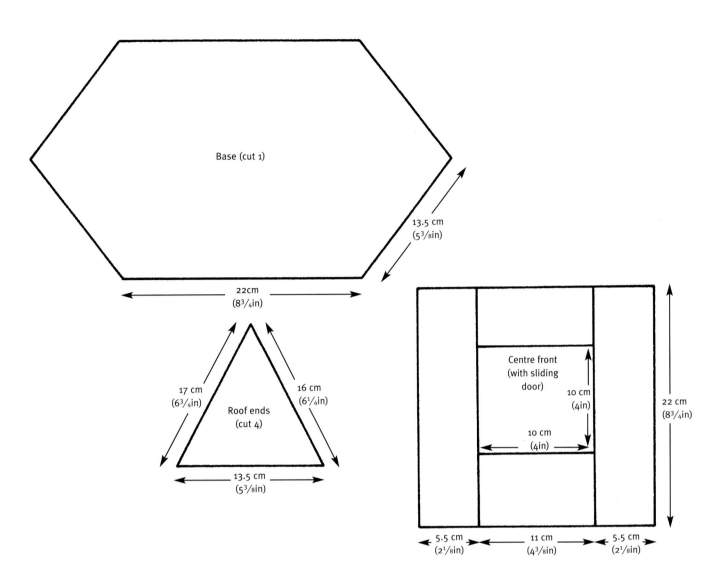

Base (cut 1)

13.5 cm
(5³/₈in)

22cm
(8³/₄in)

17 cm
(6³/₄in)

16 cm
(6¹/₄in)

Roof ends
(cut 4)

13.5 cm
(5³/₈in)

Centre front
(with sliding
door)

10 cm
(4in)

10 cm
(4in)

22 cm
(8³/₄in)

5.5 cm
(2¹/₈in)

11 cm
(4³/₈in)

5.5 cm
(2¹/₈in)

11 Secure roof pieces in place with H came between each piece. Hold in position with masking tape.

12 Slide corner came on to apex of roof and solder all joins.

13 Cut door piece with either a straight or curved top edge. The door should slide easily up and down in the brass C came.

Your terrarium is now complete. If you can add a wooden base it will enhance it even further and make it easier to carry from one place to another.

HELPFUL HINT

You can use corner came on all the leaded parts of the terrarium if you like, because you will be able to alter the angle slightly.

Designing traditional panels using came

I have drawn a few designs as suggestions for panels using came. Scale them up to the size you require (use the squaring method described on page 67). You will enjoy designing your own panels.

A FEW POINTS TO REMEMBER

- Try to avoid having small sections in your design: the came covering the small pieces of glass will hide too much of the coloured glass and spoil the overall effect of the design.

- Too many joins at one point will mean lots of blobs of solder which will make the whole panel look untidy.

- Try to keep the design at the top right-hand corner flexible and not too complicated in order to be able to allow for any adjustment in size (accommodating slight errors in cutting).

- Bear in mind the weight of the finished panel and provide for tie bars (metal bars fixed into brickwork or wood surrounds) where necessary. Came of design must lie under the tie bar to allow for copper wires (ties) to be soldered on before being twisted over the bar and secured.

Note New on the market and suitable for the hobbyist:
Rebar – a pre-tinned steel bar for reinforcing windows and panels (available in 10 x 3mm [$^3/_8$ x $^1/_8$in] and 12.5 x 3mm [$^1/_2$ x $^1/_8$in]), eliminating the need for copper wires: you solder the bar directly to your lead-came or copper-foil seams.

Rebar bender – a bench-mounted device with which to bend Rebar to specific shapes so that you can follow the pattern in your window, eliminating the need for straight strengthening bars cutting through your pattern.

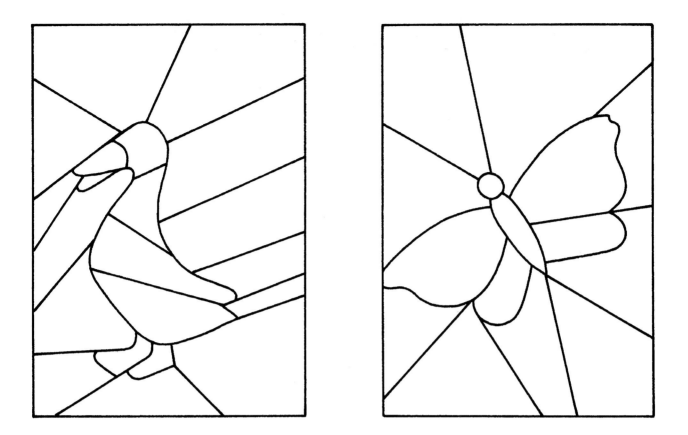

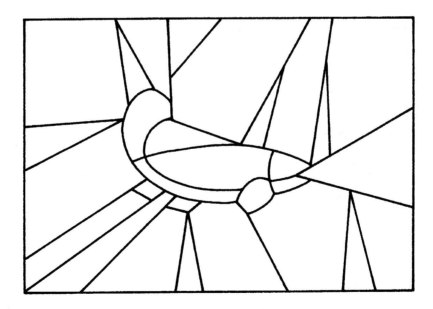

Designing for lead came

DON'T

DO

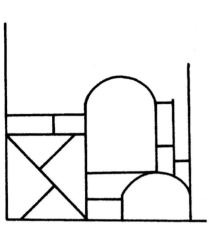

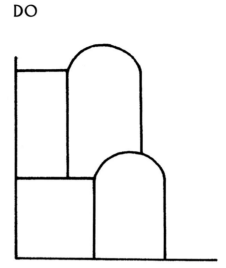

create designs which do not balance

balance the shapes

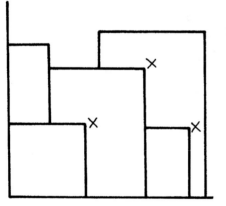

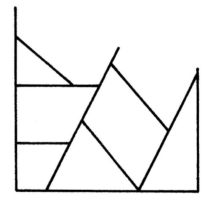

have patterns where one line of came does not continue to another line of came

continue each came line to meet another came line

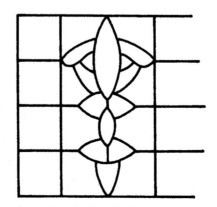

complicate your designs

keep your design simple

DON'T

DO

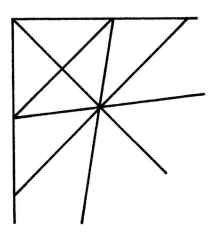

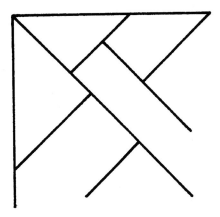

make several joins at any one point

stagger joins

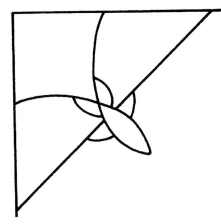

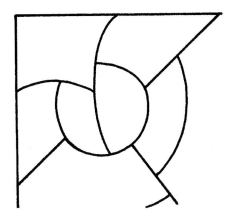

*make the design with very small pieces –
they will be hidden by the came*

make the design with large bold pieces

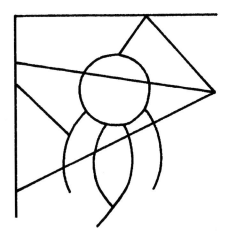

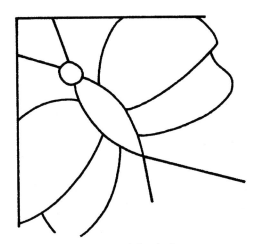

ignore design in relation to the lines of lead

make lead lines part of the design

Advanced designing for stained glass using copper-foil

When designing copper-foiled stained glass, the same principles apply as for designing for lead came work, with a few crucial differences:

- Foil can be used to cover very small pieces of glass and is more flexible than came.

- It is much easier to use foil for three-dimensional objects. (Tiffany lampshades show how copper foil can be used to its best advantage, making it possible to work on moulds using hundreds of very small pieces of glass.)

- Small terrariums and suncatchers are best made with copper-foil. Use came for terrariums with a capacity larger than about 42.5 litres (1½ cubic ft) – foil will not support the combined weight of glass plus earth.

Advanced designing for stained glass using lead came

HELPFUL HINT

If you are designing for stained glass which is to be painted and fired, the came lines need not outline the main subject as precisely as when came only is to be used – the details will be defined by painted lines.

When you have designed panels with abstract forms and simple leaf and petal patterns, the obvious progression is to design panels using more definable shapes – including the human figure, animals, flowers, landscapes and seascapes.

Study all these subjects and decide, first of all, which type you would like to work on. Then draw a few rough sketches until you are satisfied with the balance of the layout.

A PICTURE OF A DEER AND A WOMAN IN EIGHTEENTH-CENTURY COSTUME

1 Draw several sketches of the deer and then transfer your preferred sketch into a cartoon suitable for lead-came work.

2 Remove all small lines such as shading, grass, clouds, eyes etc.

3 Extend all the outlines of deer to meet the outline of another feature (the line of the back leg is carried on to meet the top of the back, the head is a continuous line and the ears are separate units).

4 Break up some of the remaining sections which otherwise would be too large (all four legs are thus segmented and the neck divided from the body at a suitable point).

5 For the background – empty at the moment – first extend all the came lines already drawn for the deer (see where the line is carried on from the ears and the tail).

6 When all lines from your main subject have been continued in this manner, break up the remaining background with lines in keeping for the picture – in this case horizontal lines at the bottom describe the ground, while higher diagonal lines denote clouds. You can treat the lady in costume in exactly the same way.

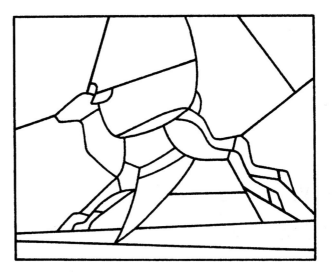

Hints, tips and reference

O nce you have begun to make desirable objects in stained glass you will want to complete them in the best way possible – giving them hooks for hanging, hinges for opening and so on. You will also need to be able to calculate appropriate angles and dimensions. This section sets out to give you a few basic ideas.

How to attach a hinge

There are two main methods for putting hinges on boxes. I have found that method 1 is easier for large boxes and method 2 better for smaller ones. However, experiment to see which you prefer. For either method you will need brass tubing (easily purchased from craft shops) and copper wire to thread through it.

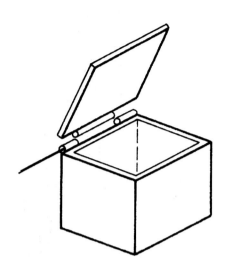

Method one. The brass tubing is cut into three pieces and attached separately to the lid and to the back of the box, with the copper wire threaded through it.

METHOD ONE

1 Cut a piece of brass tubing exactly the length of the lid. Insert the wire into the tubing to stop the tube being crushed when it is sawn.Cut it into three pieces: if the lid is 10cm (4in) long, 2 pieces 2cm (⅞in) long and 1 piece 6cm (2¼in) long.

2 Solder the longer piece to the lid – centrally (see diagram).

3 Place the lid on the box and, having positioned the smaller pieces of tubing so that the wire will go through these and also through the tube already soldered to the lid (see diagram), tape them to the back of the box. Remove both the wire and the lid.

4 Solder the smaller pieces of tubing to the box, being careful not to get solder into the open ends of the tubing.

5 Place the lid on the box and slide the wire through.

METHOD TWO

For this method it is necessary to leave the two side seams of the box unsoldered where the hinge is to be fitted.

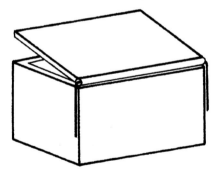

Method two. The tubing is soldered to the lid while the wire, after being passed through it, is soldered to the side seams of the box.

1 Cut the brass tubing to the length of lid and tack solder the tubing to the lid.

2 Seam solder completely, taking care not to get solder into the open ends of the tubing.

3 Thread the copper wire through the tube leaving an excess of 2cm (¾in) at each end of the box.

4 Place the lid on the box and secure with masking tape. Bend the ends of the copper wire down the sides of the box flush with the unsoldered side seams (see diagram).

5 Spot solder. Remove tape and check for fit. Completely solder the wire into the side seams, being careful not to solder the lid to the box.

6 Apply black patina and polish to all seams. Clean as for terrariums.

How to attach hanging hooks

There are several satisfactory ways of attaching hooks to a panel, although you should always bear in mind that glass and came are heavy, so that your hooks have to be firmly attached to your work.

METHOD ONE
Solder tinned copper-wire hooks to the outside of the C came at the side of the completed panel, scraping the surface off both the came and the wire before fluxing and applying solder.

METHOD TWO
Before you start to assemble your panel, make a hole in the C came with a bradawl (or a small-gauge, sharp-pointed steel knitting needle) about 5cm (2in) down each side piece. Twist a piece of wire around a pencil to form a loop. Push the ends, which should be at least 25mm (1in) long, through the hole from the outside. Flatten the ends along the came on the inside and solder securely. Then proceed with assembly as before.

For copper-foil work (see below) lay the two pieces of extended wire along the existing foiled edges and solder securely.

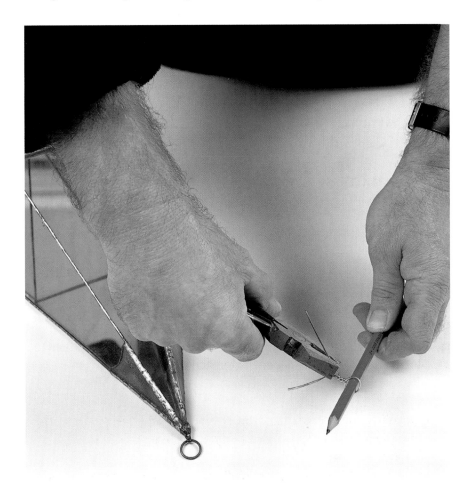

How to attach a vase cap

Attaching the vase cap is one of the most tedious things about making a lampshade.

There are two basic ways of doing this: first by glass pieces abutting the edge of the vase cap and, secondly, by fitting the vase cap over the top of the shade. The first method is most suitable to dome and cone shapes, while the second is best used with panel shapes.

There is a third method – only suitable for hanging shades – which requires no soldering at all.

METHOD ONE

1 Scrape the surface off the edge of your vase cap at the spot where it is to be soldered.

2 Cover the remainder of the vase cap with vaseline and/or masking tape to prevent the solder from spreading over the vase cap where it is not wanted. (It is not easy to clean off.)

3 Generously flux the scraped edge of the vase cap and the copper-foiled or leaded edges of the lampshade where the vase cap is to be attached. Solder the join, letting the solder flow evenly between joins.

4 Turn the lampshade over and solder on the inside, being quite generous with the solder as it will help to strengthen the connection.

5 Remove the masking tape and wash away the residue of flux and vaseline with a warm washing-up solution.

METHOD TWO

1 Scrape the inside of the vase cap where the lampshade is to be soldered to it, and apply flux to both the inside of the vase cap and the top of the shade.

2 Turn your lampshade upside down and position inside the vase cap. Employ an extra pair of hands to help you to hold it, and drop on just enough blobs of solder to hold the vase cap in place. Turn the shade the right way up to check that vase cap is correctly positioned. If you are satisfied that it is not tilted to one side, turn the shade upside-down again and solder generously the outside of the vase cap where it meets the vertical soldered lines of your lampshade.

HELPFUL HINT

I personally find it better, when soldering on vase caps, to use a paste flux rather than a liquid flux. Experiment to discover your own preference.

METHOD THREE
This is not used very often as it lacks the strength provided by the soldering in methods 1 and 2.

1 Use two equally sized vase caps fractionally larger than the top of your shade.

2 Place one vase cap inside the shade and one on top of it.

3 Put a small length of threaded rod through the lower vase cap, then the shade, and finally the top vase cap. Secure the nuts underneath and on top.

ADDING WIRE SUPPORTS TO YOUR SHADE
If you think your shade needs extra strength add wire supports as follows:

1 Turn lampshade upside-down into a cardboard box – to hold it in position.

2 Measure around the bottom edge of shade to ascertain length of wire required. Cut tinned copper wire (16- or 18-gauge is suitable) with tin snips to the required length.

3 Flux rim of shade. Use paste flux in preference to liquid flux – this latter tends to run down inside the shade if too much is used.

4 Pull the wire through the paste flux and lay it on the top fluxed rim of shade, securing it in a few places with masking tape. Solder over the top until it resembles a beaded seam.

5 If it is an open-topped shade, do the same at the top rim of the shade. (If the shade has a vase cap attached this will add strength to the shade.)

6 If you feel that the shade needs even more support, add another wire about 2.5cm (1in) up from the base inside the shade. Spot solder where the wire touches any foiled seams.

ATTACHING A SPIDER TO YOUR LAMPSHADE
An open-topped lampshade needs either a spider or a strong metal bar (with central hole) to support it.

1 You can buy either three- or four-pronged spiders, so choose the one which best suits your shade.

2 Bend the prongs using a vice, so that they lie flush with the inside of your shade and, if possible, along a downward soldering line. Flux and solder the spider prongs to this downward soldered line (or seam).

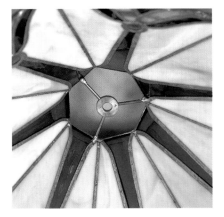

HELPFUL HINT
It is possible to make your own spider using brass rods and metal washers, but I recommend buying a ready-made one since this is much simpler.

How to make your own lampshade mould with papier mâché

MATERIALS

Old newspapers (not magazines)

Heavy-duty wallpaper paste (only a small amount is used, but the paste will keep indefinitely in powder form)

White emulsion paint

A hanging-basket liner made of fibre, not plastic (obtainable from any good garden centre). The liner will give you a good foundation with which to start

Although you do not need a mould if you want to make a panel-shaped lampshade, you will need one to make either a dome-shaped or cone-shaped Tiffany shade. Lampshade moulds are quite expensive to buy, but it is reasonably easy to make your own with papier mâché. I experimented to see if there were any household objects that might serve as a mould for a shade, and I found that a hanging-basket liner was ideal for the purpose.

METHOD

1 Tear the newspaper into strips about 5cm (2in) wide. Never cut the paper, as the rough edges of torn paper will help to bind the strips together when you are making your mould: the easiest way to tear the paper is to pull it along a ruler. Tear up a good supply of strips because when you start pasting you will not want to stop to tear up more paper.

2 Mix the wallpaper paste in an old washing-up bowl or something similar. You only need a weak solution.

3 Turn your hanging basket liner upside down and sit it on a few sheets of newspaper. If the liner has a flat bottom, screw up a sheet of newspaper and place it on the flat base so that you end up with a softly rounded top for your shade.

4 Pull a strip of paper through the paste and put it over the screwed-up ball of newspaper and down each side of your basket liner. Place another strip at right angles to the first and then build up the number of strips, spreading them evenly around the the top of the liner, until the ball of newspaper is really secure. Keep all the strips of newspaper well moistened with the paste.

5 When you are satisfied that the shape at the top is correct, start to cover the remainder of the liner. Paste strips horizontally, starting from the base. Overlap each piece by about 3mm ($\frac{1}{8}$in). Then paste pieces diagonally over the complete form until you have three layers of newspaper covering the complete liner. The liner by itself has sufficient strength to support your work. Turn the mould round and check that the shape is even all round, measuring down from the centre of the top to the base using a tape measure.

6 Allow the mould to dry thoroughly (about two days at normal room temperature). Then apply a coat of white emulsion paint.

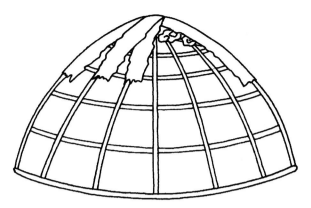

Strips of paper about 5cm (2 in) wide are applied over screwed-up newspaper to give the shade a rounded top

When the shape is correct, paste strips of newspaper horizontally, starting from the base

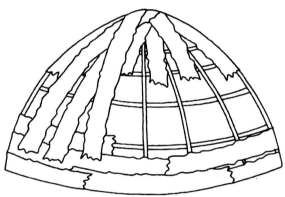

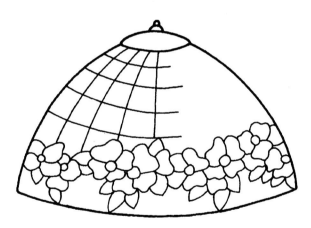

After drying (which takes up to two days) your design can be drawn on to the mould

7 Drill a hole in the centre at the top for your threaded rod. (If you do not have a drill, it is possible to make the hole with a sharp pair of scissors – and patience!)

8 Your mould is now complete. And it has an added advantage because you can, if you wish, draw your design directly onto it. When you have completed your shade, you can simply apply a fresh coat of emulsion and you are ready to draw your next design.

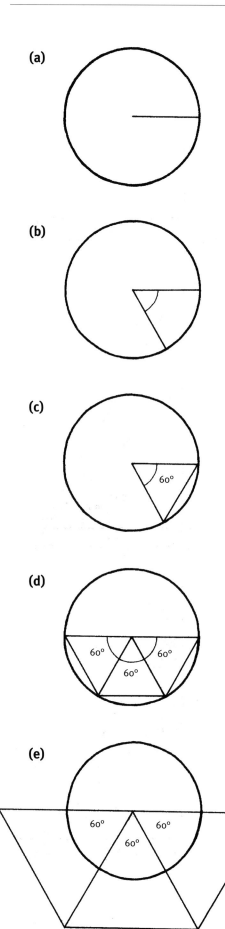

(a)

(b)

(c)

(d)

(e)

HINTS ON CALCULATIONS

HOW TO DESIGN A POLYGONAL BASE FOR A TERRARIUM

1 Draw a circle (any size).

2 Find the centre and draw a line from the centre to the circumference **(diagram a)**.

3 For a six-sided base, with the aid of a protactor, mark an angle of 60° from the first line and draw a second line from the centre to the circumference **(diagram b)**.

4 Join the two points on the circumference **(diagram c)**.

5 Measure the distance between these two points. Using this measurement, mark around the circumference where the remaining four (three) corners of the base will fall, checking that all your angles are 60°. Join the points on the circumference to complete your figure **(diagram d)**.

6 It is very easy to make your base larger: simply extend the lines radiating from the centre further than the circumference, measure an equal distance along each line and join the marks **(diagram e)**.

Note For a five-sided base, you should use an angle of 72° at the centre, and for an octagonal (eight-sided) base the angle should be 45°.

HOW TO DESIGN A PANELLED LAMPSHADE

Before anything else you will need to decide on how many panels you want your shade to have and what size you want it to be – you will need to know the diameter at both the top and bottom of the shade. Remember to choose a size for which you can easily buy a vase cap.

For a six-panelled shade with a diameter of 5cm (2in) at its top and 28cm (11in) at its bottom:

1 Draw a circle with a diameter the same as you want for the bottom of the shade, that is 28cm (11in).

2 Follow steps 1–5 of the instructions for creating a polygonal base. You now have the base measurement (16cm [6½in]) for one of your panels.

3 To calculate the slope and height of your panel: draw a line A–B half the length of your diameter (14cm [5½in]) and draw a line A–C at right angles to this line at A **(diagram i)**.

4 Using a protractor, draw a line B–D at an angle of 60° to line A–B from B. You now have the length of your panel **(diagram ii)**.

5 To calculate the top measurement of your panel, draw a circle 5cm (2in) in diameter - that is, the same as the diameter of the top of your shade. Follow steps 1–5 of the instructions for creating a polygonal base. You will find that the top measurement of each of your six panels should be 54mm (2⅛in).

6 Divide the top measurement by two (27mm/1¹/₁₆in). Draw a line measuring 27mm (1¹/₁₆in) from line A–C to line B–D (parallel to line A–B). You now have a drawing of half your panel **(diagram iii)**. To complete your pattern piece, draw a mirror image of this half with line A–D as the foldline.

For an eight-panelled shade of the same dimensions, follow steps 1–3 of the instructions for a six-panelled shade. Then, with the aid of a protractor, draw a line B–E at an angle of 45° to line A–B from B **(diagram ii)**.

7 If your eight-panelled shade – like your six-panelled shade – is to measure 5cm (2in) at the top, next draw a line measuring 27mm (1¹/₁₆in) from line A–C to B–E, which will be half the top edge of your panel **(diagram iii)**.

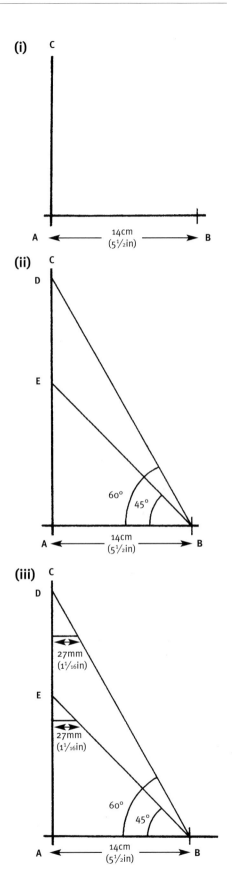

ABOUT THE AUTHOR

Mary Shanahan was a talented artist, who taught both stained glass techniques and watercolour painting, and was a founding member of the local art society in her home town of Molesey in Surrey, England.

Sadly, Mary died in July 2000, shortly after completing this book and before the first proofs were ready for her to see. She leaves a son, Murray, and young grandchildren Kerry and Liam, for whom these brilliantly coloured projects will be a small but fitting memorial to a warm and vibrant personality.

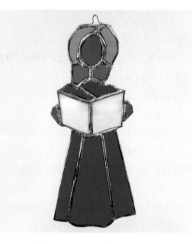

INDEX

OTHER CRAFT TITLES BY GMC PUBLICATIONS

American Patchwork Designs in Needlepoint
Melanie Tacon
A Beginners' Guide to Rubber Stamping
Brenda Hunt
Blackwork: A New Approach
Brenda Day
Celtic Cross Stitch Designs
Carol Phillipson
Celtic Knotwork Designs
Sheila Sturrock
Celtic Knotwork Handbook
Sheila Sturrock
Celtic Spirals and Other Designs
Sheila Sturrock
Collage from Seeds, Leaves and Flowers
Joan Carver
Complete Pyrography
Stephen Poole
Contemporary Smocking
Dorothea Hall
Creating Colour with Dylon
Dylon International
Creative Doughcraft
Patricia Hughes
Creative Embroidery Techniques Using Colour
Through Gold
Daphne J. Ashby & Jackie Woolsey
The Creative Quilter: Techniques and Projects
Pauline Brown
Decorative Beaded Purses
Enid Taylor
Designing and Making Cards
Glennis Gilruth
Glass Engraving Pattern Book
John Everett
Glass Painting
Emma Sedman

How to Arrange Flowers: A Japanese
Approach to English Design
Taeko Marvelly
How to Make First-Class Cards
Debbie Brown
An Introduction to Crewel Embroidery
Mave Glenny
Making and Using Working Drawings for
Realistic Model Animals
Basil F. Fordham
Making Character Bears
Valerie Tyler
Making Decorative Screens
Amanda Howes
Making Fairies and Fantastical Creatures
Julie Sharp
Making Greetings Cards for Beginners
Pat Sutherland
Making Hand-Sewn Boxes: Techniques and
Projects
Jackie Woolsey
Making Knitwear Fit
Pat Ashforth & Steve Plummer
Making Mini Cards, Gift Tags & Invitations
Glennis Gilruth
Making Soft-Bodied Dough Characters
Patricia Hughes
Natural Ideas for Christmas: Fantastic
Decorations to Make
Josie Cameron-Ashcroft & Carol Cox
Needlepoint: A Foundation Course
Sandra Hardy
New Ideas for Crochet: Stylish Projects for
the Home
Darsha Capaldi
Patchwork for Beginners
Pauline Brown

Pyrography Designs
Norma Gregory
Pyrography Handbook (Practical Crafts)
Stephen Poole
Ribbons and Roses
Lee Lockheed
Rose Windows for Quilters
Angela Besley
Rubber Stamping with Other Crafts
Lynne Garner
Sponge Painting
Ann Rooney
Stained Glass: Techniques and Projects
Mary Shanahan
Step-by-Step Pyrography Projects for the
Solid Point Machine
Norma Gregory
Tassel Making for Beginners
Enid Taylor
Tatting Collage
Lindsay Rogers
Temari: A Traditional Japanese Embroidery
Technique
Margaret Ludlow
Theatre Models in Paper and Card
Robert Burgess
Trip Around the World: 25 Patchwork,
Quilting and Appliqué Projects
Gail Lawther
Trompe l'Œil: Techniques and Projects
Jan Lee Johnson
Wool Embroidery and Design
Lee Lockheed

The above represents a small selection of titles currently published or scheduled to be published.
All are available direct from the publishers or through bookshops, newsagents and specialist retailers.
To place an order, or to obtain a complete catalogue, contact:

GMC Publications,
Castle Place, 166 High Street, Lewes, East Sussex BN7 1XU, United Kingdom
Tel: 01273 488005 Fax: 01273 478606
E-mail: pubs@thegmcgroup.com

Orders by credit card are accepted